Object-Oriented PHP

Writing Resilient & Reusable Code in PHP 7

Junade Ali

Object-Oriented PHP

Writing Resilient & Reusable Code in PHP 7

Junade Ali

ISBN 978-0-244-90350-3

Associated source code files for this book are available over Git and can be found by visiting https://ju.je/object-orientedphp-book-code online.

Contents

Introduction

After finishing my previous book "Mastering PHP Design Patterns", I suddenly felt as if I had lost a major activity for transatlantic flights. I have never been a fan of on-board Wi-Fi, there is undoubtably a huge amount of writing that can be achieved in the 12 hours of disconnect between London Heathrow and San Francisco International, especially if you're an insomniac.

There is however, a far more important reason for writing this book. I recently published a blog post regarding containing some PHP Interview Questions, containing a list of interview questions/answers that senior PHP Developers who work on Enterprise grade software should be able to answer. A number of people then reached out to me asking good material where they could learn the fundamentals of Object Oriented Programming whilst working with PHP. I searched, but failed to find a book on PHP Object Orientation that I could confidently recommend, so I decided to write my own.

This book will seek to cover the fundamentals of Object Oriented Programming strictly within the context of PHP. This book will be written in PHP 7, due to the fact that this version of PHP introduced a number of features which are incredibly useful when writing Object Oriented code.

Going beyond the basics, we'll cover more detailed topics such as Dependency Injection, SOLID Principles and Design Patterns. We'll also cover how you can use some open-source tools to improve the reliability of your software and using detect bad practice within your codebase.

I am a great believer in teaching my demonstration, this book will work on the same principle. Each chapter will try to be as self-contained on the topic as possible and heavily supported with code examples, if there is a concept or language feature you struggle with, please run the code example and have a play around. Try and break the code and see what's gone wrong, and then try and fix it.

Purpose

Sometimes it is easier to write badly written code than well-written code, indeed it may even be faster to do so at the start of a project. However, code which is badly written gets harder to change as time goes on and the design deteriorates; well-designed code, however, remains relatively easy to adjust and add new features to. Fundamentally, bad code stops a business being able to react to forces of change.

Recently we've heard Agile being used as a Project Management buzzword a lot, but behind the buzz there is a fundamentally sound principle. Agile software development is rooted in the ability for a project to react to changing requirements and ultimately deliver value on a more reliable basis. However, in order to successfully implement Agile, your code must be resilient to the forces of change, you must be able to re-design your code mid-flow such that a change in feature can be elegantly implemented into your codebase. This is fundamentally the business benefit of having well-designed code; resiliency and increased speed of delivering new functionality.

If you're an experienced developer, chances are you've seen teams rewrite bad code for what eventually becomes equally bad code. You've likely seen the staff-churn from developers quitting over having to work long hours in stressed environments whilst struggling to deliver code. Whilst not a book on refactoring, this book seeks to describe the best practise approaches for Object-Oriented software development, allowing you to ensure that your code is resilient to the forces of change and your codebase can grow as easily today as it did yesterday.

The key to writing well-written code in modern PHP is a sound understanding of Object-Orientation - this book seeks to marry the theory behind Object-Orientation and how you can practically implement this in PHP 7. This book does not seek to be a PHP 101 book, but seeks to build on your existing experience to introduce new patterns and practises into your workflow.

Conventions

This book is written to version 7 and above of the PHP language, the reason for this is that there are some significant changes and improvements in PHP 7 as to how Object Orientation is implemented.

In many cases this book will be written in the format of a tutorial from chapter to chapter, the source code is available on GitHub and can be accessed by visiting `https://ju.je/object-orientedphp-book-code`

Where's the UML?

Traditionally, books on Object-Oriented Programming will be filled with UML diagrams. This was a convention I broke previously in my last book and it is indeed a convention I intend to continue to break throughout this book.

As Agile software development practices become more common, large upfront design is becoming a relic of the past. Whilst deployment diagrams are still in use, it's rare to see a team of developers pondering a UML class diagram.

This is a book about Object-Oriented Programming *in PHP*, therefore we have already established a common language for us to share ideas through. I can write PHP which you can read, take apart and play with. There is no need to add additional complexity by communicating ideas through yet another language.

Code Style

PHP is presented as follows:

```
1   <?php
2   echo "hello";
```

Shell scripts will be indicated as follows:

```
1   echo "192.168.99.100  project.local" >> /etc/hosts
```

Command line inputs and outputs will be marked as follows:

```
1   # dig A google.com +short
2   216.58.204.78
```

Please note that # marks a privileged shell and $ marks an unprivileged shell

Errata and Comments

Errata will be handled promptly, and can be emailed to me directly at mjsa@junade.com.

Back to Basics

This first chapter aims to be a self-contained introduction to the language features that allow us to use Object-Orientation in modern PHP. We'll set-up a basic PHP project and walk through some some OOP (Object-Oriented Programming) principles. Along the way, we'll stumble on some other bits of non-OOP knowledge that will benefit you through the course of this book.

We'll be working inline with PHP 7 in this book, so if you want to follow along, make sure your PHP installation is at a minimum of 7.0.

Composer Package Manager

Let's get started with our first project. A key tool to grasp the use of is Composer, a Dependency Manager for PHP. Using Composer we can include third-party libraries into our codebase and also perform Autoloading, which we'll discuss later.

Using third-party code in your codebase a very good idea in a lot of cases. There are developers who insist on building their own everything, they fundamentally adopt a world view that everything is better if they build it themselves; this is referred to "Not Invented Here" Syndrome. This outlook can prove to be problematic for a number of reasons; external implementations have often be scrutinised and refined to an extent your own never will be. Additionally building your own implementations of things that are commonly used by other developers can lead to a maintenance burden. It is often to extend a library that does 95% of what you want it to do, rather than build your own. Composer allows us to effectively manage external dependencies and the manage which versions of those dependencies we pull in.

Instead of us having to copy and paste classes into our codebase, or use PEAR, Composer offers us a fairly elegant way of managing project dependencies and their versions. If you come from a JavaScript background you'll find it similar to NPM.

Installing Composer

In order to get started, we need to have Composer installed on our system. You can install Composer on Mac or Linux by running the following commands on your system. For installing the current version of Composer on my Mac, I ran the following commands:

```
1  curl -sS https://getcomposer.org/installer | php
2  sudo mv composer.phar /usr/local/bin/
```

Further information about Composer alongside how you can install and use it on Windows, is available at getcomposer.org.

After you have installed Composer, you should be able to run composer within the terminal or Command Prompt.

Creating our Project

We can interactively set-up our composer.json file running composer init in our project directory. This will then open an interactive prompt from where we can configure our composer dependencies. At the very bottom we'll see a preview of the JSON that will be written to our composer.json file and then we can confirm it's creation.

```
                          1 — -bash — 80×31
[Junades-MacBook-Pro-7:1 junade$ composer init                          ]


    Welcome to the Composer config generator



This command will guide you through creating your composer.json config.

Package name (<vendor>/<name>) [junade/1]: icyapril/one
Description []: Chapter 1 of PHP OOP book.
Author [Junade Ali <junade@              >, n to skip]: n
Minimum Stability []:
Package Type (e.g. library, project, metapackage, composer-plugin) []: project
License []:

Define your dependencies.

Would you like to define your dependencies (require) interactively [yes]? no
Would you like to define your dev dependencies (require-dev) interactively [yes]
? no

{
    "name": "icyapril/one",
    "description": "Chapter 1 of PHP OOP book.",
    "type": "project",
    "require": {}
}

Do you confirm generation [yes]? yes
Junades-MacBook-Pro-7:1 junade$ 
```

After this process, the file will be written to the current working directory. The next step is to enable Autoloading in this project.

PSR-4 Autoloading

In PHP it is possible to manually include one PHP file into another using `require`, `require_once`, `include` and `include_once`. This approach can often lead to difficulty in managing all the different classes around a project and can also add difficulties when you want to add new classes to a project.

Instead, it is possible to use a tactic known as Autoloading - this will dynamically manage detecting and including PHP files as they're added, renamed and removed.

We'll cover what PSR standards are in a later section, but there are currently two PSR standards surrounding Autoloading: PSR-0 and PSR-4. Here we will cover the latest of these standards, PSR-4, using the implementation included in Composer.

In order to utilise PSR-4 Autoloading, we need to amend the `composer.json` file that has been created for us. Currently, the JSON looks pretty bare:

```
1  {
2      "name": "icyapril/one",
3      "description": "Chapter 1 of PHP OOP book.",
4      "type": "project",
5      "require": {}
6  }
```

We can add an autoload property to our JSON, such as the following:

```
1  {
2    "autoload": {
3      "psr-4": {
4        "IcyApril\\ChapterTwo\\": "src/"
5      }
6    }
7  }
```

In this example, `IcyApril` is the Vendor namespace, whilst `ChapterTwo` is a sub-namespace. Technically only the Vendor namespace is required - but we can add one or more sub-namespaces as required to further organize our code. Note that we must add a namespace separator (\\) after our namespace value, else Composer will throw an error.

The value of `src/` represents the directory where the code files we want to autoload actually live on the file system.

Combined, our `composer.json` looks something like this:

```
 1  {
 2    "name": "icyapril/one",
 3    "description": "Chapter 1 of PHP OOP book.",
 4    "type": "project",
 5    "require": {},
 6    "autoload": {
 7      "psr-4": {
 8        "IcyApril\\ChapterTwo\\": "src/"
 9      }
10    }
11  }
```

Let's run composer update and we're good to move forward.

```
[Junades-MacBook-Pro:1 junade$ composer update
Loading composer repositories with package information
Updating dependencies (including require-dev)
Nothing to install or update
Generating autoload files
Junades-MacBook-Pro:1 junade$
```

You'll also notice a composer.lock file has been created by Composer, be sure to commit this on any version control system you're using. This file contains the exact versions of all the dependencies you're using, so when someone downloads this project and runs composer install, they can be confident their dependencies are at the same version as yours.

Namespaces

Namespaces allow us to divide our code into separate named sections. You can think about it like putting files in folders on your computer, it is easier to manage files when split into folders and subfolders, instead of all being in one folder.

As discussed in the previous section, it is a necessity to split out code into namespaces in order to take advantage of PSR-4 autoloading. In this section, I'll give a brief overview of how Namespaces work inside this set-up.

Firstly, let's create a class to take advantage of PSR-4 autoloading. Firstly, let's create a src directory, within this new folder let's create a file called Dog.php. To this file, I'll add the following code:

```php
<?php

namespace IcyApril\ChapterTwo;


class Dog
{
    public function talk(): string
    {
        return "Woof!";
    }
}
```

In the first line, I've declared that this class lives in the `IcyApril\ChapterTwo` namespace. The `Dog` class which is then declared also lives in this namespace and accordingly the `talk()` function can be accessed from the global namespace using `\IcyApril\ChapterTwo\Dog();`.

We can demonstrate this works by writing the following to our `index.php` in the root directory of this project:

```php
<?php

require_once('./vendor/autoload.php');

$oscar = new \IcyApril\ChapterTwo\Dog();

echo $oscar->talk() . PHP_EOL;
```

The first `require_once` statement calls in our Autoload file that Composer has generated for us to utilise PSR-4 autoloading. The next line is where we instantiate the class Dog as the $oscar variable.

Classes

By instantiating the class we are effectively creating a new object based on the class. The class simply acts as a template for what the object should be, but an object has it's own instance outside of a class.

A class acts as a logical entity, whereas an object is a physical entity, for example; we can have a class named Dog which outlines what a dog is. Oscar, a pet dog, is instead a object. Whilst the concept of a Dog is a logical entity, Oscar is actually a physically entity which we can cuddle and feed.

A class named Dog explains what a dog is, the class is merely a blueprint. The object assigned to the variable $oscar is the physical object.

Whilst our Dog class currently only outlines a method called talk(), it is possible for the class to also outline properties (variables) the class can hold. Let's suppose we want to keep a count of the amount of times the talk() function is run.

I've amended the Dog class to contain a $talkCount property and a getTalkCount() function:

```php
1   <?php
2
3   namespace IcyApril\ChapterTwo;
4
5
6   class Dog
7   {
8       private $talkCount = 0;
9
10      public function talk(): string
11      {
12          $this->talkCount++;
13          return "Woof!";
14      }
15
16      public function getTalkCount(): int
17      {
18          return $this->talkCount;
19      }
20  }
```

We define a property called $talkCount with a default value of 0 using private $talkCount = 0;. Alternatively we could define a property without a default value using private $talkCount;.

We are then able to complete a simple function called getTalkCount() to return the value of the $talkCount property. We can alter our index.php file to include a simple for() loop that allows us to demonstrate the behaviour of the class:

```php
1   <?php
2
3   require_once('./vendor/autoload.php');
4
5   $oscar = new \IcyApril\ChapterTwo\Dog();
6
7   for ($talk = 1; $talk <= 10; $talk++) {
8       echo $oscar->talk() . ' ' . $oscar->getTalkCount() . PHP_EOL;
9   }
```

Inside the for() loop we call the talk() function from the $oscar object and proceed to get the value of the getTalkCount() function:

```
[Junades-MacBook-Pro:1 junade$ php index.php
Woof! 1
Woof! 2
Woof! 3
Woof! 4
Woof! 5
Woof! 6
Woof! 7
Woof! 8
Woof! 9
Woof! 10
Junades-MacBook-Pro:1 junade$ 
```

Visibility

So why did we make our $talkCount property private?

A method or property being marked as private means it can only be accessed by methods within the class. If we replaced private with public we would be able to access the property externally from the object, so we would be able to get the value from the instantiated object using `echo $oscar->talkCount;`. Additionally, you can set the value externally of the object by doing `$oscar->talkCount = 5;`.

We don't want to allow people to alter the `talkCount` variable, just view what the number is. In order to do this, we create a public `getTalkCount()` method which returns the value of the variable, but we provide no way for someone set the variable. Similarly, we can provide for validation when setting a variable, or manipulate data we return by using similar setter and getter methods.

Other than `private` or `public` we can set visibility to `protected`. Later on, we'll discuss how it's possible to extend classes through inheritance, when a property or method is marked as `private` subclasses cannot access them. In order to make a property or method visible to subclasses but not visible externally - you can use the `protected` option.

Scalar Types Hinting

You may have noticed the `: int` or the `: string` after a given method in the class we defined above, this is something known as Scalar Type Hinting. We outline exactly what type of value we want to return. Other than `int` and `string`, we can also use `bool` and `null`. The ability to specifically do this type of type hinting is unique to PHP 7. Additionally we can use other types of Type Hinting, whether we want to specify we want to return an `array` or an object from a particular class or interface.

Not only can we use this in return types, we can also use this in the parameters a given method accepts. For example, I've created a new class in a file called `Food.php`, the code is below:

```php
1   <?php
2
3   namespace IcyApril\ChapterTwo;
4
5
6   class Food
7   {
8       private $food;
9
10      public function __construct(string $food)
11      {
12          $this->food = $food;
13      }
14
15      public function getFood(): string
16      {
17          return $this->food;
```

```
18        }
19  }
```

The constructor (__construct()) accepts a string and sets this to the private variable $food, we then return this value when the getFood method is called.

I've now added a new method to our Dog.php file which accepts an object of type Food and will return a string saying what's been eaten.

```
1  public function feed(Food $food): string
2  {
3      return "Eaten: " . $food->getFood();
4  }
```

We can put this all together by appending the following to our index.php:

```
1  $dogFood = new \IcyApril\ChapterTwo\Food("Dog Food");
2  echo $oscar->feed($dogFood) . PHP_EOL;
```

Now when we run our index.php file, we will get an output indicating that Oscar has eaten Dog Food:

```
Junades-MacBook-Pro:1 junade$ php index.php
Woof! 1
Woof! 2
Woof! 3
Woof! 4
Woof! 5
Woof! 6
Woof! 7
Woof! 8
Woof! 9
Woof! 10
Eaten: Dog Food
Junades-MacBook-Pro:1 junade$
```

Static Methods

It is possible to make methods and properties in a class accessible without instantiating an object. This can be done by setting the methods to be static.

Inside our Dog.php class, I've added a new static property called $legCount:

```
1   private static $legCount = 4;
```

Additionally, I've added a static method which returns the leg count of a dog:

```
1   public static function legCount(): int
2   {
3       return self::$legCount;
4   }
```

Note that from a static method, we must use self to call or modify other static methods or properties, as the class is not instantiated we cannot use $this.

We can access this property using the Scope Resolution Operator (::) instead of the usual object access operator (->). The Scope Resolution operator is sometimes referred to as Paamayim Nekudotayim in the PHP core (literally, Hebrew for "double colon"), this was introduced by the Israel-based Zend company (who help contribute to the open-source PHP core).

We can call our legCount() method by appending the following to our index.php file:

```
1   echo "Dogs have " . \IcyApril\ChapterTwo\Dog::legCount() . " legs." . PHP_EOL;
```

With this now in place, our new index.php yields a response like this:

```
Junades-MacBook-Pro:1 junade$ php index.php
Woof! 1
Woof! 2
Woof! 3
Woof! 4
Woof! 5
Woof! 6
Woof! 7
Woof! 8
Woof! 9
Woof! 10
Eaten: Dog Food
Oscar has 4 legs.
Junades-MacBook-Pro:1 junade$
```

Note that as of PHP 7, accessing a static property non-statically is deprecated. Similarly accessing a non-static property statically is also deprecated.

Interfaces

Interfaces allow us to define what methods or properties a given class should have and what properties they should accept.

They allow us to group classes of a type together, for example we can bind a Cat and Dog class together using a Mammal interface.

Let's suppose we want all mammals to have the talk, feed and legCount methods, we can create an interface which looks like this:

```php
1   <?php
2
3   namespace IcyApril\ChapterTwo;
4
5
6   interface Mammal
7   {
8       public function talk(): string;
9
10      public function feed(Food $food): string;
11
12      public static function legCount(): int;
13  }
```

We can ensure our Dog class implements the Mammal interface by making sure the class is declared as class Dog implements Mammal instead of merely class Dog.

Let's now build out a Cat class which complies with the interface we built. Let's start off by declaring the class with no methods:

```php
1   <?php
2
3   namespace IcyApril\ChapterTwo;
4
5
6   class Cat implements Mammal
7   {
8
9   }
```

Let's try to instantiate the Cat class in our index.php, we can do this by adding $whiskers = new \IcyApril\ChapterTwo\Cat(); to our index.php file. However, if we try and run this without declaring the methods we defined in our Mammal interface, we will get an error like this as soon as we hit that line in our code:

```
Woof! 5
Woof! 6
Woof! 7
Woof! 8
Woof! 9
Woof! 10
Eaten: Dog Food
Dogs have 4 legs.
PHP Fatal error: Class IcyApril\ChapterOne\Cat contains 3 abstra
ct methods and must therefore be declared abstract or implement t
he remaining methods (IcyApril\ChapterOne\Mammal::talk, IcyApril\
ChapterOne\Mammal::feed, IcyApril\ChapterOne\Mammal::legCount) in
 /Users/junade/Desktop/phpBook2/code/1/src/Cat.php on line 11

Fatal error: Class IcyApril\ChapterOne\Cat contains 3 abstract me
thods and must therefore be declared abstract or implement the re
maining methods (IcyApril\ChapterOne\Mammal::talk, IcyApril\Chapt
erOne\Mammal::feed, IcyApril\ChapterOne\Mammal::legCount) in /Use
rs/junade/Desktop/phpBook2/code/1/src/Cat.php on line 11
Junades-MacBook-Pro:1 junade$ 
```

As you can see, if we specify that a class implements a given interface, we have to implement the methods and properties defined in that interface. Let's build out the class:

```php
<?php

namespace IcyApril\ChapterTwo;


class Cat implements Mammal
{
    private static $legCount = 4;

    public function talk(): string
    {
        return "Meow.";
    }

    public function feed(Food $food): string
    {
```

```
17          return "Eaten: " . $food->getFood();
18      }
19
20      public static function legCount(): int
21      {
22          return self::$legCount;
23      }
24  }
```

By adding the following methods to our `index.php` file, we can now see this code run without issue:

```
[Junades-MacBook-Pro:1 junade$ php index.php
Woof! 1
Woof! 2
Woof! 3
Woof! 4
Woof! 5
Woof! 6
Woof! 7
Woof! 8
Woof! 9
Woof! 10
Eaten: Dog Food
Dogs have 4 legs.
Meow.
Junades-MacBook-Pro:1 junade$
```

Whilst they may seem unnecessary right now, Interfaces are a vital part of Object-Orientation and a powerful tool for clean code. In next chapter we'll learn how we can utilise these with Polymorphism to improve the quality of our code.

Abstract Classes

If you look at both our `Cat` and `Dog` classes, you'll notice both the `feed()` and `legCount()` functions are the same.

We can therefore turn our `Mammal` interface into an abstract class. An abstract class is like an interface, but can also contain methods which have implementations (i.e. a body to the method). Like an interface, an abstract class simply cannot be instantiated.

We start off by replacing `interface Mammal` with `abstract class Mammal`.

In an interface, all methods defined cannot contain implementation, hence why can define methods like this `public function talk(): string;`. However, for a method to contain no body in an abstract class, we must define the method as abstract by doing `public abstract function talk(): string;`.

We can now move over complete methods for the `feed` and `legCount` methods to the new abstract class.

After this is done, our new abstract class is ready to go:

```php
1   <?php
2
3   namespace IcyApril\ChapterTwo;
4
5   abstract class Mammal
6   {
7       private static $legCount = 4;
8
9       public abstract function talk(): string;
10
11      public function feed(Food $food): string
12      {
13          return "Eaten: " . $food->getFood();
14      }
15
16      public static function legCount(): int
17      {
18          return self::$legCount;
19      }
20  }
```

Inheritance

So how do we now actually use this class? Well, an abstract class is a type of class instead of an interface implementation.

Accordingly, in our Cat class - we need to substitute `class Cat implements Mammal` with `class Cat extends Mammal`.

Having now abstracted the `feed` and `legCount` methods away to an abstract class, we can remove these methods from our `Cat` class.

```php
<?php

namespace IcyApril\ChapterTwo;


class Cat extends Mammal
{
    public function talk(): string
    {
        return "Meow.";
    }
}
```

We can also do the same for our `Dog` class:

```php
<?php

namespace IcyApril\ChapterTwo;


class Dog extends Mammal
{
    private $talkCount = 0;

    public function talk(): string
    {
        $this->talkCount++;

        return "Woof!";
    }

    public function getTalkCount(): int
    {
        return $this->talkCount;
    }
}
```

Having now eliminated duplicate code, through allowing code reuse via an abstract method, we can now re-run this code to see it works as before:

```
[Junades-MacBook-Pro:1 junade$ php index.php                    ]
Woof! 1
Woof! 2
Woof! 3
Woof! 4
Woof! 5
Woof! 6
Woof! 7
Woof! 8
Woof! 9
Woof! 10
Eaten: Dog Food
Dogs have 4 legs.
Meow.
Junades-MacBook-Pro:1 junade$ ▯
```

Inheritance with Normal Classes

Here we've used inheritance with an abstract class, but it is also possible to do inheritance with normal classes.

Aegean is a breed of cat, suppose it makes a different "meow" to what we've put in our main Cat class. We can create a separate AegeanCat class which overrides our Cat class.

Our new class extends the existing Cat class but overrides the talk() method with a different one. Instead of talk() returning "Meow." like our Cat class does, our AegeanCat class will return "Meeeooowww.":

```php
1   <?php
2
3   namespace IcyApril\ChapterTwo;
4
5
6   class AegeanCat extends Cat
7   {
8       public function talk(): string
9       {
10          return "Meeeooowww.";
11      }
12  }
```

We can now test this method by adding the following to our index.php file:

```php
1   $felix = new \IcyApril\ChapterTwo\AegeanCat();
2   echo $felix->talk() . PHP_EOL;
```

Nothing too special here, just instantiating the AegeanCat class and running the talk() method. This is what the output looks like:

```
[Junades-MacBook-Pro:1 junade$ php index.php
Woof! 1
Woof! 2
Woof! 3
Woof! 4
Woof! 5
Woof! 6
Woof! 7
Woof! 8
Woof! 9
Woof! 10
Eaten: Dog Food
Dogs have 4 legs.
Meow.
Meeeooowww.
Junades-MacBook-Pro:1 junade$ 
```

The Final Keyword

There may be times you want to prevent a class being inherited. This is where the final keyword comes into play. When a class definition is prefixed with the word final, a fatal error is triggered if you then try to extend that class.

Earlier, we went ahead and extended our Cat class with an AegeanCat class. Suppose we were to open up our Cat class and change class Cat extends Mammal to final class Cat extends Mammal, our class would now look like this:

```php
1   <?php
2
3   namespace IcyApril\ChapterTwo;
4
5
6   final class Cat extends Mammal
7   {
8       public function talk(): string
9       {
10          return "Meow.";
11      }
12  }
```

With our class defined as `final`, let's try and re-run our `index.php` file and see what happens when we get to the point where we try and instantiate our `AegeanCat` class:

```
Woof! 2
Woof! 3
Woof! 4
Woof! 5
Woof! 6
Woof! 7
Woof! 8
Woof! 9
Woof! 10
Eaten: Dog Food
Dogs have 4 legs.
Meow.
PHP Fatal error:  Class IcyApril\ChapterOne\AegeanCat may not inh
erit from final class (IcyApril\ChapterOne\Cat) in /Users/junade/
Desktop/phpBook2/code/1/src/AegeanCat.php on line 17

Fatal error: Class IcyApril\ChapterOne\AegeanCat may not inherit
from final class (IcyApril\ChapterOne\Cat) in /Users/junade/Deskt
op/phpBook2/code/1/src/AegeanCat.php on line 17
Junades-MacBook-Pro:1 junade$
```

As you can see we get a fatal error indicating that our `AegeanCat` class may not inherit from final class `Cat`.

We can also ensure that individual methods cannot be overridden by prefixing them with the word final. In our Cat class, let's define our talk() function as a final method.

This time, let's mark the talk method in our Cat class as final. We can do this by changing public function talk(): stringto final public function talk(): string:

```php
1   <?php
2
3   namespace IcyApril\ChapterTwo;
4
5
6   class Cat extends Mammal
7   {
8       final public function talk(): string
9       {
10          return "Meow.";
11      }
12  }
```

This time when we reach the part of our index.php file that tries to instantiate the AegeanCat class, we get an error indicating that we cannot override the final method talk() within the Cat class in the AegeanCat class:

```
                         1 — -bash — 65×20
Woof! 2
Woof! 3
Woof! 4
Woof! 5
Woof! 6
Woof! 7
Woof! 8
Woof! 9
Woof! 10
Eaten: Dog Food
Dogs have 4 legs.
Meow.
PHP Fatal error:  Cannot override final method IcyApril\ChapterOn
e\Cat::talk() in /Users/junade/Desktop/phpBook2/code/1/src/Aegean
Cat.php on line 17

Fatal error: Cannot override final method IcyApril\ChapterOne\Cat
::talk() in /Users/junade/Desktop/phpBook2/code/1/src/AegeanCat.p
hp on line 17
Junades-MacBook-Pro:1 junade$ 
```

Coding Standards

How do you write your PHP? Do you put your brackets on a new line? How do you camel-case your variables?

Inconsistencies in code standardisation can result in code that is inconsistent from developer-to-developer. This lack of uniformity can result in a slower development pace and also incompatibility between projects and libraries. Fortunately the PHP Interop Group exist to try and resolve these gaps in standardisation.

The PHP Framework Interop Group (PHP-FIG) is formed of representatives from various PHP projects who discuss how various PHP projects can work better together and standardise commonalities. Together, they come up with PHP Standards Recommendations (PSRs) which are worked on and revised until they become "Accepted" at which point they can be referenced as finalised.

From time-to-time standards are updated inline with modern developments. Whilst PSR-0 represented the original autoloading standards, this was later superseded by PSR-4 which we discuss in this book. Once superseded the legacy PSR can be marked as "Deprecated". Standards can also work on a complementary basis, for example PSR-1 is a "Basic Coding Standard" whilst PSR-2 acts as a "Coding Style Guide".

Standardisation is by no way unique to PHP, those of you familiar with networking may have heard of Internet Drafts and RFCs published by the Internet Engineering Task Force. Those of you familiar with Java may have heard of Java Specification Requests which describe proposed standards and specifications for Java technology.

PSR-1 and PSR-2

I would highly recommend adopting PSR-1 and PSR-2 in your projects without alteration. It allows others to be able to collaborate on your codebase easily, inline with widely accepted standards. Some developers choose to alter the specifications in line with their other preferences - I am of the view this is a regressive approach and not sensible. It slows down the ability for developers to quickly pick up projects whilst also making it harder to switch from project-to-project. Your code can be uniquely poetic to you, whilst still adopting a widely accepted coding style.

Setting PSR-1 and PSR-2 in PHPStorm

For those of you lucky enough to use PHPStorm as your IDE, you can set it to comply with the PSR Standards in your Preferences pane (under `PHPStorm > Preferences` on Mac or `File > Settings` on Windows/Linux). Firstly navigate to `Languages & Frameworks > Editor > Code Style`.

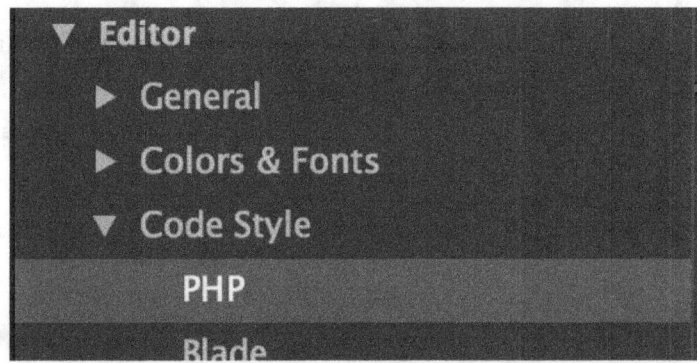

From here, you will see a "Set from..." option in the top-right of the resulting setting pane allowing you to set PSR-1/PSR-2 as the given style.

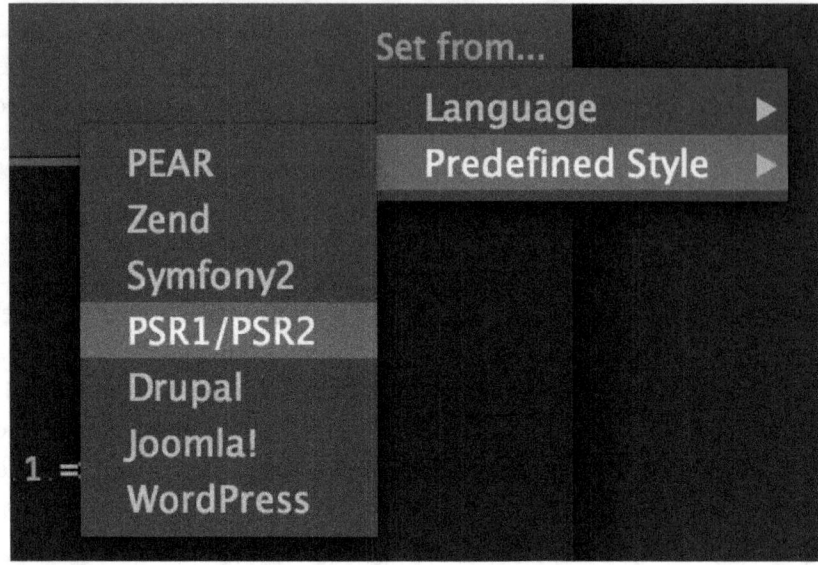

You can then reformat code by clicking on Code > Refactor Code or using the keyboard shortcut Alt + Command + L on a Mac or Ctrl + Alt + L on a PC.

Other Editors

Other editors have support for bringing code inline with PSR standards, though you may need to pull in an external dependency or two to do it.

Users of other editors may want to pull in PHP_CodeSniffer or PHP-CS-Fixer. Users of the Atom editor may have milage with PHP-fmt.

If you have a Continuous Integration workflow, validating code is formatted can be done as part of your build process.

Conclusion

In this chapter we learnt the basics of doing Object-Orientation with PHP; we covered how classes and objects work and how property visibility can be controlled, whilst covering interfaces, abstract classes alongside inheritance. Alongside setting up a Composer project, we also learnt about the PSR coding styles and how PSR-4 affects Autoloading.

In the next chapter we'll build upon this understanding by diving deeper into some more advanced Object-Orientation and cover some best practice approaches.

Before proceeding, make sure you understand all the concepts explained here - go back and play with the code examples if need be. When you're ready, let's proceed.

Advanced Concepts

In the last chapter we deep-dived into the core concepts of Object-Orientation - but Object-Orientation is more than just classes and objects. In this chapter, we'll be using these concepts in practical examples.

Magic Methods

Just before we get into the full flow of this chapter, I wanted to briefly explain what the phrase "magic method" means. In the previous chapter you will have seen that we have expressed constructors as a __construct() function. This is an example of a magic method.

In PHP magic methods are special functions in class that are automatically called when certain behaviour happens in a program. For example, in PHP you can clone an object using the clone keyword: $dolly = clone $sheep;. If a function called __clone() exists in the $sheep object, this will be run before the object is cloned. Similarly, if you try and echo an object you'll find the __toString() magic method being run to decide what the output should be.

Let me briefly demonstrate this, suppose we have a Person class that looks like this:

```php
1   <?php
2
3   class Person
4   {
5       private $name;
6
7       public function __construct(string $name)
8       {
9           $this->name = $name;
10      }
11
12      public function __toString(): string
13      {
14          return "Hello! My name is " . $this->name . ".";
15      }
16  }
```

Note the __toString() Magic Method returns a given string. Using this, we can build an index.php file to utilise this:

```php
1    <?php
2
3    require_once('Person.php');
4
5    $bob = new Person('Bob');
6
7    echo $bob . PHP_EOL;
```

What we've done is instantiated the Person class and just echoed out the output we get back. As you can see from the output, we get the value of the _toString() method:

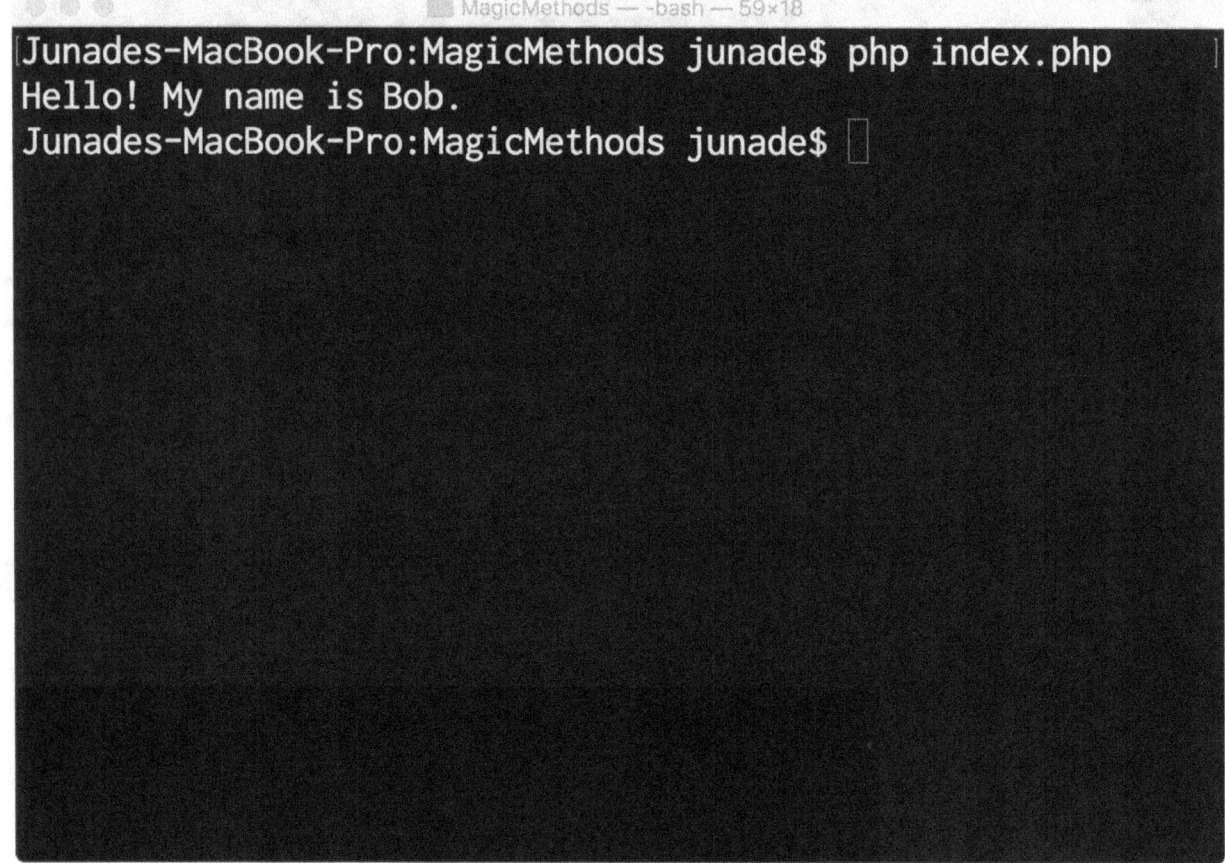

If you're curious, without the __toString() Magic Method, you would get a string conversion error if you tried to echo an object:

```
[Junades-MacBook-Pro:MagicMethods junade$ php index.php
PHP Recoverable fatal error:  Object of class Person could
not be converted to string in /Users/junade/Desktop/phpBook
2/code/3/MagicMethods/index.php on line 12

Recoverable fatal error: Object of class Person could not b
e converted to string in /Users/junade/Desktop/phpBook2/cod
e/3/MagicMethods/index.php on line 12
Junades-MacBook-Pro:MagicMethods junade$
```

There are many other Magic Methods which are useful in PHP, for example; if __debugInfo() exists, it will be called you dump the output of an object using var_dump(). Similarly, if a method is inaccessible (i.e. doesn't exist) and you have a __call() method, that function will be run instead.

Polymorphism

When we talk about Polymorphism, in the context of PHP, we're almost always referring to Subtype Polymorphism. Subtype Polymorphism is a lengthy term for quite a simple concept, let me explain. Over the course of this book, so far, we're encountered lots of interfaces - interfaces fundamentally allow us to treat multiple classes with different underlying methods with the same Interfaces. Polymorphism utilises this such that we can treat different classes as one by utilises a common interface.

In short: Polymorphism is a pattern in Object-Oriented Programming where classes can share a common interface, whilst having different underlying behaviour.

For example, let's suppose we have an interface called Region for geographical areas:

```php
1   <?php
2
3   interface Region
4   {
5       public function __construct(string $name);
6
7       public function getInfo(): string;
8   }
```

This is a very basic structure, a constructor which allows us to set a place name and a function to getInfo() about the region. Let's implement this in a City class:

```php
1   <?php
2
3   class City implements Region
4   {
5       private $name;
6
7       public function __construct(string $name)
8       {
9           $this->name = $name;
10      }
11
12      public function getInfo(): string
13      {
14          return $this->name . " is a city.";
15      }
16  }
```

Very simple, let's repeat this a few times, with a Town class:

```php
1   <?php
2
3   class Town implements Region
4   {
5       private $name;
6
7       public function __construct(string $name)
8       {
9           $this->name = $name;
10      }
11
```

```
12      public function getInfo(): string
13      {
14          return $this->name . " is a town.";
15      }
16  }
```

Finally, once more with a Village class:

```
1   <?php
2
3   class Village implements Region
4   {
5       private $name;
6
7       public function __construct(string $name)
8       {
9           $this->name = $name;
10      }
11
12      public function getInfo(): string
13      {
14          return $this->name . " is a village.";
15      }
16  }
```

Now, let's try something different in our index.php file, let's instantiate these classes but keep the objects inside an array called $regions. We then can iterate through them using a foreach() loop and run the getInfo() function on each object.

```
1   <?php
2
3   require_once('Region.php');
4   require_once('City.php');
5   require_once('Town.php');
6   require_once('Village.php');
7
8   $regions = [
9       new City('London'),
10      new Town('Rugby'),
11      new City('New York'),
12      new Village('Dunchurch'),
13      new Town('Lutterworth'),
```

```
14        new City('Baltimore'),
15        new City('San Francisco')
16   ];
17
18   foreach ($regions as $region) {
19        echo $region->getInfo() . " \n";
20   }
```

As you can see, we're running the getInfo() method on every object in the $regions array, as every object in the $regions array shares the same interface (and therefore has a getInfo() method). We are able to run the same method on every object because of polymorphism.

The output of our index.php file looks like this:

```
Junades-MacBook-Pro:Polymorphism junade$ php index.php
London is a city.
Rugby is a town.
New York is a city.
Dunchurch is a village.
Lutterworth is a town.
Baltimore is a city.
San Francisco is a city.
Junades-MacBook-Pro:Polymorphism junade$
```

When we inject one class into another, we can Type Hint the name of the interface, from this point onwards a client class doesn't need to know anything about how a class works - we know what methods to use and that's all that counts. This makes our class more modular and extendable.

When operating a car, you don't need to know what's going on behind the scenes - you know where the controls are and that's all you need. As a car driver, you have a general interface as to know how a car works, and you can apply this knowledge to all different types of cars. That's fundamentally what Polymorphism is about.

Dependency Injection

A key principle to understand in this chapter is Dependency Injection, in other words injecting one object into the constructor when instantiating another.

In the last Chapter we saw an example of constructing a class with a string:

```php
1   <?php
2
3   class Food
4   {
5       private $food;
6
7       public function __construct(string $food)
8       {
9           $this->food = $food;
10      }
11
12      public function getFood(): string
13      {
14          return $this->food;
15      }
16  }
```

Let's create a class called Lunch which uses Dependency Injection with the Food object.

```php
1   <?php
2
3   class Lunch
4   {
5       private $main;
6       private $dessert;
7
8       public function __construct(Food $main, Food $dessert)
9       {
10          $this->main    = $main;
11          $this->dessert = $dessert;
12      }
13
```

```
14        public function getMenu(): array
15        {
16            return [
17                'main'   => $this->main->getFood(),
18                'desert' => $this->dessert->getFood()
19            ];
20        }
21    }
```

When we want to use our Lunch class, we need to pass in instances of the Food class into the constructor. Once these are passed in, they are stored within the instance of Lunch and the methods or properties can be accessed from there.

Putting this all together, we need instances of the Food class ready to inject into our Lunch class when we instantiate it.

```
1   <?php
2
3   require_once('Food.php');
4   require_once('Lunch.php');
5
6   $tacos = new Food('Tacos');
7   $cake  = new Food('Cake');
8
9   $lunch = new Lunch($tacos, $cake);
10
11  var_dump($lunch->getMenu());
```

When we execute the above code, this is the response we get the following output:

```
[Junades-MacBook-Pro:DependencyInjection junade$ php index.php ]
array(2) {
  ["main"]=>
  string(5) "Tacos"
  ["desert"]=>
  string(4) "Cake"
}
Junades-MacBook-Pro:DependencyInjection junade$ ⬚
```

That's all there is to Dependency Injection, all we're doing is passing objects into constructors when creating other objects. We could inject anything from database handlers to API clients, but this is a very powerful principle.

How not to do it: Singletons

The temptation for many developers has been to utilise a pattern known as the Singleton. This pattern works by creating an object that can only be instantiated once throughout the application. It effectively becomes an object with a global state.

This pattern effectively works by hacking a class that can only be instantiated once and cannot be duplicated about.

There are many ways to implement this pattern, but here's an example Singleton class:

```php
1    <?php
2
3    final class Singleton
4    {
5        private $random;
6
7        /**
8         * Singleton constructor.
9         *
10        * Private so it cannot be constructed externally.
11        */
12       private function __construct()
13       {
14           $this->random = rand(0, 1000);
15       }
16
17       /**
18        * Prevent cloning (by making the method private).
19        */
20       private function __clone()
21       {
22       }
23
24       /**
25        * Prevent serialize.
26        */
27       private function __sleep()
28       {
29       }
30
31       /**
32        * Prevent unserialize.
33        */
34       private function __wakeup()
35       {
36       }
37
38       /**
39        * Call this method to get singleton
40        */
41       public static function instance(): Singleton
42       {
```

```
43        static $instance = false;
44        if ($instance === false) {
45            // Late static binding (PHP 5.3+)
46            $instance = new static();
47        }
48
49        return $instance;
50    }
51
52    public function returnSomething(): string
53    {
54        return "Something " . $this->random;
55    }
56 }
```

When this class is instantiated, we are setting a random value between 1 and 1000 in the constructor and when the returnSomething() function is called that random value is returned. The instance() function is a static method which returns an instance of the class, this is the same instance each time. Here's a script which will demonstrate this:

```
1  <?php
2
3  require_once('Singleton.php');
4
5  $first = Singleton::instance();
6  echo $first->returnSomething() . PHP_EOL;
7
8  $second = Singleton::instance();
9  echo $second->returnSomething() . PHP_EOL;
```

As the instance() method returns the same instance regardless of how many times the method is run. In order to demonstrate this, when we run the script above, we will see the following output:

```
Junades-MacBook-Pro:Singleton junade$ php index.php
Something 109
Something 109
Junades-MacBook-Pro:Singleton junade$ ▯
```

As you can see, the random number generated when the Singleton was instantiated, and returned by the returnSomething() function, is the same for both the $first and $second object.

Dependency Injection Containers

Dependency Injection Containers are a tool which can help when implementing Dependency Injection. You do not need to use Dependency Injection Container software to perform Dependency Injection, but it makes the task easier. In order to use Dependency Injection Containers, you'll need a container library (like PHP-DI).

When performing Dependency Injection manually, you need to first create the objects before you instantiate them. For example, you could do:

```
1  <?php
2  $db = new CoolMySQLClient('host', 'root', 'pass');
3  $users = new Users($db);
4
5  $users->getAll();
6  ?>
```

However, with a Dependency Injection Container, you can use the container to get the object automatically:

```
1  $users = $container->get('Users');
```

You can also configure what class the container uses for a given interface. So in the case above, CoolMySQLClient implements the DBInterface interface. So whenever the container sees a dependency that type hints for DBInterface, it will inject CoolMySQLClient with the constructor variables we request:

```
1  $container->set('DBInterface', \DI\object('CoolMySQLClient'))->constructor('host\
2  ', 'root', 'pass');
```

There are many Dependency Injection Containers around, if you're interested in learning the specifics of how you can use one in your code - be sure to check out some of the documentation pages on PHP-DI which you can find at php-di.org[1]. There is also a project called Pimple (by Symfony) which can be found at pimple.sensiolabs.org[2].

Generators

In PHP, functions can only ordinarily return one value. This is where generators come into play, generators are essentially functions that return multiple values, the results can then be iterated over using functions like foreach(). Whilst functions stop running after they reach the return keyword, generators can keep running whilst yielding data.

Generators are implemented much like any other function, except for the fact they use yield instead of the return keyword. Here is an example:

---

[1]http://php-di.org/
[2]http://pimple.sensiolabs.org/

```php
1   <?php
2
3   function squareNumbers()
4   {
5       for ($i = 1; $i <= 10; $i++) {
6           yield pow($i, 2);
7       }
8   }
9
10  $numbers = squareNumbers();
11
12  foreach ($numbers as $number) {
13      echo $number . "\n";
14  }
```

This is how the output looks when we run that script:

```
Junades-MacBook-Pro:Generators junade$ php index.php
1
4
9
16
25
36
49
64
81
100
Junades-MacBook-Pro:Generators junade$
```

You can use this in classes too, we'll demonstrate this later in this chapter in the section on "Composition in the Real World".

Composition vs Inheritance

Let's suppose we are building a people-management system for a school. In this example we have 4 fundamental classes. There are Student and Teacher classes and a Human class that contains the properties shared by both. Additionally, there is another class called HeadTeacher which represents the Head Teacher.

Inheritance

At the top of the food chain we might have an abstract class called Person and then have concrete implementations for different types of people in a school..

Inheritance is fundamentally a "is a" relationship. A Student is a Person. Similarly a HeadTeacher is a Teacher which is a Person.

Our Person class can look something like this:

```php
<?php

abstract class Person
{
    protected $name;
    protected $house;

    /**
     * Person constructor.
     *
     * @param String $name
     * @param String $house
     *
     * @throws Exception
     */
    public function __construct(string $name, string $house)
    {
        if ($this->validateName($name) === false) {
            throw New Exception('Name must contain at least 2 segments.');
        }

        if ($this->validateHouse($house) === false) {
            throw New Exception('Invalid house.');
        }

        $this->name  = $name;
```

```
27          $this->house = $house;
28      }
29
30      /**
31       * Check name contains at least 2 parts.
32       *
33       * @param String $name
34       *
35       * @return bool
36       */
37      private function validateName(string $name): bool
38      {
39          $nameSegments = explode(" ", $name);
40
41          if (count($nameSegments) < 2) {
42              return false;
43          }
44
45          return true;
46      }
47
48      /**
49       * Check if a house is valid.
50       *
51       * @param String $house
52       *
53       * @return bool
54       */
55      private function validateHouse(string $house): bool
56      {
57          $validHouses = ['Griffindor', 'Slytherin', 'Hufflepuff', 'Ravenclaw'];
58
59          if (in_array($house, $validHouses)) {
60              return true;
61          }
62
63          return false;
64      }
65
66      /**
67       * Gets a persons house.
68       *
```

```
69        * @return String
70        */
71       public function getHouse(): string
72       {
73           return $this->house;
74       }
75   }
```

We have a basic structure for what a Person looks like as an abstract class, properties such as a name and a house within the school are set. As this is just an abstract class in order for someone to actually take advantage of the methods, someone must actually instantiate a child class.

Our Student and Teacher classes can simply extend the Person class:

```
1   <?php
2
3   class Teacher extends Person
4   {
5       public function teach(string $subject): string
6       {
7           return "Teaching: " . $subject;
8       }
9   }
```

Our HeadTeacher can in turn extend our Teacher class:

```
1   <?php
2
3   final class HeadTeacher extends Teacher
4   {
5       public function createRule(string $rule): string
6       {
7           return date("Y-m-d h:i:sa") . ": " . $rule;
8       }
9   }
```

The Teacher class can add additional methods to the Person class and the HeadTeacher class can add additional methods to the Teacher class. We can instantiate these concrete classes as we need them.

Imagine, however, you then get asked to create a Student who can teach, maybe a Prefect, how does that fit into the Inheritance hierarchy? This is one of the difficulties when using Inheritance. In this instance, we could consider abstracting the teach() method away to the PersonObject, but this then means there are plenty of objects with the teach() that don't need them. Similarly we can consider making a Trait that contains the teach() method and sharing that around, however this is still not ideal.

This is where Composition comes into play, instead of building our objects on a hierarchy, we build objects what functionality they can do (using Dependency Injection).

Composition

Composition differs from inheritance because we are talking about a "has a" relationship instead of the "is a" relationship we find with inheritance.

In order to do this, we will use Dependency Injection. Our Person class becomes a class we can inject into our Teacher or Student class. Our Teacher class can in turn be embedded into our HeadTeacher class.

This time, instead of our Person class being abstract, it is a concrete class:

```php
<?php

class Person
{
    protected $name;
    protected $house;

    /**
     * Person constructor.
     *
     * @param String $name
     * @param String $house
     *
     * @throws Exception
     */
    public function __construct(String $name, String $house)
    {
        if ($this->validateName($name) === false) {
            throw New Exception('Name must contain at least 2 segments.');
        }

        if ($this->validateHouse($house) === false) {
            throw New Exception('Invalid house.');
        }

        $this->name = $name;
```

```php
27          $this->house = $house;
28      }
29
30      /**
31       * Check name contains at least 2 parts.
32       *
33       * @param String $name
34       *
35       * @return bool
36       */
37      private function validateName(String $name): bool
38      {
39          $nameSegments = explode(" ", $name);
40
41          if (count($nameSegments) < 2) {
42              return false;
43          }
44      }
45
46      /**
47       * Check if a house is valid.
48       *
49       * @param String $house
50       *
51       * @return bool
52       */
53      private function validateHouse(String $house): bool
54      {
55          $validHouses = ['Griffindor', 'Slytherin', 'Hufflepuff', 'Ravenclaw'];
56
57          if (in_array($house, $validHouses)) {
58              return true;
59          }
60
61          return false;
62      }
63
64      /**
65       * Gets a persons house.
66       *
67       * @return String
68       */
```

```
69       public function getHouse(): string
70       {
71           return $this->house;
72       }
73   }
```

When it comes to us building our Teacher method, we can simply use Dependency Injection to include an instance of the Person class. When we want to expose certain methods of the Person class in the Teacher class, we can simply create methods that encapsulate the methods of the Person class, additionally we can add any other methods we require. Here's what it looks like all together:

```
1    <?php
2
3    class Teacher
4    {
5        private $person;
6
7        public function __construct(Person $person)
8        {
9            $this->person = $person;
10       }
11
12       public function teach(string $subject): string
13       {
14           return "Teaching: " . $subject;
15       }
16
17       public function getHouse(): string
18       {
19           $this->person->getHouse();
20       }
21   }
```

In a similar light, we can build out our HeadTeacher class, I've made a few differences though. Instead of constructing the class with a Person object, we instead use an instance of the Teacher class. Also note that I've chosen not to expose the teach() method in the HeadTeacher class despite it being a public method in the Teacher class:

```php
1   <?php
2
3   class HeadTeacher
4   {
5       private $teacher;
6
7       public function __construct(Teacher $teacher)
8       {
9           $this->teacher = $teacher;
10      }
11
12      public function createRule(string $rule): string
13      {
14          return date("Y-m-d h:i:sa") . " " . $rule;
15      }
16
17      public function getHouse(): string
18      {
19          $this->person->getHouse();
20      }
21  }
```

We can demonstrate this behaviour with an `index.php` file that looks like this:

```php
1   <?php
2
3   require_once('Person.php');
4   require_once('Teacher.php');
5   require_once('HeadTeacher.php');
6
7   $person      = new Person('Neville Longbottom', 'Griffindor');
8   $teacher     = new Teacher($person);
9   $headTeacher = new HeadTeacher($teacher);
10
11  echo $headTeacher->createRule("Thou shalt not eat sweets in the corridors.");
12  echo PHP_EOL;
```

It looks like this once executed (yes, I'm really writing this at 01:36AM on a Saturday):

```
[Junades-MacBook-Pro:Composition junade$ php index.php
2017-02-04 01:36:48am: Thou shalt not eat sweets in the corridors.
Junades-MacBook-Pro:Composition junade$ 
```

A major advantage of using composition over inheritance is the higher flexibility you get whilst dealing with components. It is more natural to build classes out of their components rather than trying to piece together a family tree that links all your components together. The quirks in parent classes can't cause bugs later down the family tree, this fundamentally means code is easier to adjust.

On the flip side, we have had to write some forwarding methods which do nothing but forward one method to the same method in a different class. This can be very verbose, however traits (containing multiple forwarding methods shared across multiple classes) and magic methods (forwarding dynamically with the __call() method) can help mitigate the effects of this with a reduced tradeoff.

This tradeoff led to a rule-of-thumb by the Gang of Four that developers should "Composition over Inheritance". To be clear; this doesn't mean "Composition *instead of* Inheritance", it just means that it most cases Composition is the more sensible route to go down (with exceptions).

Composition in the Real World

Let's suppose we're building a basic program that can either read blog entries from a JSON file and outputs them to the screen. The entries can either be text entries or link entries. We have one script that displays the links in the file and another which output text posts.

We have a JSON file that contains an array of objects. The objects have two properties type and value. The type can either be text or link, and the value is either actual value of the text or the link. Our JSON file looks something like this:

```
 1  [
 2    {
 3      "text": "junade.com",
 4      "type": "link"
 5    },
 6    {
 7      "text": "It's raining today.",
 8      "type": "text"
 9    },
10    {
11      "text": "icyapril.com",
12      "type": "link"
13    },
14    {
15      "text": "Hello world!",
16      "type": "text"
17    }
18  ]
```

We accordingly build a simple class that can read data from the JSON file, the class contains two methods getData() and getDataByType(), note that in development you'd want to add some error checking into the mix (in case the JSON file was corrupted):

```
 1  <?php
 2
 3  class JSON
 4  {
 5      private $data;
 6
 7      public function __construct(string $file)
 8      {
 9          $this->processFile($file);
10      }
11
12      private function processFile(string $file)
13      {
14          $contents    = file_get_contents($file);
15          $array       = json_decode($contents);
16          $arrayReverse = array_reverse($array);
```

```php
17        $this->data    = $arrayReverse;
18    }
19
20    public function getData(): array
21    {
22        return $this->data;
23    }
24
25    public function getDataByType(string $type): array
26    {
27        $result = [];
28        $data    = $this->getData();
29
30        foreach ($data as $entry) {
31            if ($entry->type === $type) {
32                array_push($result, $entry);
33            }
34        }
35
36        return $result;
37    }
38 }
```

We are now going to create some classes to read the data, let's specify what this Interface looks like:

```php
1  <?php
2
3  interface Reader
4  {
5      public function __construct(JSON $data);
6
7      public function getContent(): Generator;
8  }
```

Note that the getContent() function returns type Generator instead of a scalar type (e.g. a string), this is because generators return values of type Generator. From this Interface, we can then go ahead and make a class for getting links from a JSON file:

```php
1   <?php
2
3   class Link implements Reader
4   {
5       private $data;
6
7       public function __construct(JSON $data)
8       {
9           $this->data = $data;
10      }
11
12      public function getContent(): Generator
13      {
14          $links = $this->data->getDataByType('link');
15
16          foreach ($links as $link) {
17              yield $link->text;
18          }
19      }
20  }
```

If we wanted to make a Text class, we simply can alter the getContent() function so it looks for text blocks instead - an example of this is included in the code files. We can use the Link class by having the following script in our index.php file:

```php
1   <?php
2
3   require_once('JSON.php');
4   require_once('Reader.php');
5   require_once('Link.php');
6
7   $data = new JSON('data.json');
8   $link = new Link($data);
9
10  foreach ($link->getContent() as $content) {
11      echo $content. "\n";
12  }
```

Once we run this, we can see the URLs from our JSON file being read and output:

```
Junades-MacBook-Pro:CompositionInTheRealWorld junade$
 php index.php
icyapril.com
junade.com
Junades-MacBook-Pro:CompositionInTheRealWorld junade$
```

In real life, you will undoubtably face this example a lot. You may not be dealing with a object to read data from a JSON file, but you will when reading from a database. Whether using MySQLi, PDO or an ORM, you will have an object you need to inject into other objects in order to read data. In this instance, I would urge you to use Composition with Dependency Injection - this is demonstrably better than using Inheritance.

Traits

PHP doesn't allow for Multiple Inheritance - so we can't simple extend multiple methods in one go like this:

```php
1  <?php
2  class API extends JSON, REST
```

There are multiple reasons why PHP doesn't allow this, and it has been frequently debated in the PHP Community. PHP has a process for accepting changes to the language - it requires an RFC (Request For Comments) which must be scrutinised voted on in order for changes to be accepted.

The process is a simplified approach to the one used by the (IETF) Internet Engineering Task Force in creating standards for the internet. Instead of multiple inheritance being permitted, the PHP community sided instead with allowing a restricted version of horizontal code-reuse in the form of Traits.

Traits can be used to aid code-reuse in making sure classes converge towards open-standards. Suppose we have a product system, whereby we can create objects for products based around this interface:

```php
1  <?php
2
3  interface Product
4  {
5      public function __construct(float $purchasePrice, float $salesPrice);
6
7      public function getSalePrice(): float;
8
9      public function getPurchasePrice(): float;
10
11     public function getSalesTax(): float;
12 }
```

For example, if we have a Chocolate bar we can use the following logic:

```php
1  <?php
2
3  class Chocolate implements Product
4  {
5
6      private $purchasePrice;
7      private $salesPrice;
8
9      public function __construct(float $purchasePrice, float $salesPrice)
10     {
11         $this->purchasePrice = $purchasePrice;
12         $this->salesPrice = $salesPrice;
13
14     }
15
16     public function getSalePrice(): float
17     {
18         return $this->salesPrice+$this->getSalesTax();
19     }
```

```
20
21      public function getPurchasePrice(): float
22      {
23          return $this->purchasePrice;
24      }
25
26      public function getSalesTax(): float
27      {
28          return ($this->salesPrice * 0.2)+0.05;
29      }
30  }
```

Suppose however, that we have multiple products that use the same calculation that we have in getSalesTax(), it is possible for us to abstract this away to a Trait. Instead of vertical inheritance we can then utilise horizontal inheritance to share the function across whatever classes we want. We can start off by building a class like this:

```
1   <?php
2
3   trait StandardSalesTax
4   {
5       public function getSalesTax(): float
6       {
7           return ($this->salesPrice * 0.2)+0.05;
8       }
9   }
```

Then in order to utilise this we can adjust our Chocolate class to pull in this function:

```
1   <?php
2
3   class Chocolate implements Product
4   {
5       use StandardSalesTax;
6
7       private $purchasePrice;
8       private $salesPrice;
9
10      public function __construct(float $purchasePrice, float $salesPrice)
11      {
12          $this->purchasePrice = $purchasePrice;
13          $this->salesPrice = $salesPrice;
```

```
14
15        }
16
17        public function getSalePrice(): float
18        {
19            return $this->salesPrice+$this->getSalesTax();
20        }
21
22        public function getPurchasePrice(): float
23        {
24            return $this->purchasePrice;
25        }
26  }
```

Notice the use StandardSalesTax; line which calls in the class and also the removal of the getSalesTax() function. Note, however, that getSalesTax() remains within our Product interface, it is vital to ensure we program to abstractions rather than concrete functions (concretions).

With our StandardSalesTax Trait in place, any class can pull in getSalesTax() where it is needed. Additionally, we can create other Trait's with different tax regimes for other Product classes to pull in, and of course a Trait can contain as many methods as you need. Note that Trait's have visibility over private methods in the class you include them in.

From here, we can create a basic script to test the functionality of our Chocolate class:

```
1  <?php
2
3  require_once('Product.php');
4  require_once('StandardSalesTax.php');
5  require_once('Chocolate.php');
6
7
8  $chocolateBar = new Chocolate(0.5, 1);
9  var_dump($chocolateBar->getSalePrice());
```

Traits are a controversial concept within PHP, personally I find it is far safer to first use Dependency Injection where possible. However, should you find the need to include Traits, be sure to ensure you continue to program towards an interface instead of just concretions in a trait. Programming to interfaces rather than concretions will save you a lot of headache, particularly when using this feature.

```
Junades-MacBook-Pro:Traits junade$ php index.php
float(1.25)
Junades-MacBook-Pro:Traits junade$
```

Conclusion

In this chapter, we've built upon your basic Object-Orientation knowledge to cover a range of topics. We started by discussing Dependency Injection, a key principle to achieving Object-Orientation, and how this ties in with Polymorphism. Beyond, this we've covered the disadvantages of Singletons and discussed PHP language features such as Traits and Iterators. Going into the next chapter, we'll start to discuss the theoretical principles around Object Orientation and how they can improve your code quality.

In the next chapter, we'll cover how you can use SOLID software development principles to ensure your Object-Oriented code is well-designed, inline with the core principles of Object-Orientation.

SOLID Design Principles

There are many PHP Developers who will write "OOP" on their resumes, but they will understand little more than how to write classes and instantiate them. So far in this book we've covered some more advanced language features that help us write Object-Oriented code, however you still may be scratching your head wondering what purpose they are for. The concept of interfaces, for example, confuses many developers; why would you write classes which contain no body?

This chapter seeks to go into the fundamental principles behind Object-Oriented Programming in a clear and concise way. These principles are often referred to as the "First Five Principles of Object-Oriented Programming", or the SOLID Principles. The acronym of "SOLID" was coined by Robert C. Martin based on what Michael Feathers described as the "First Five Principles".

Single Responsibility Principle

Robert C. Martin expressed this principle quite simply: "A class should have only one reason to change."

Consider you're making a PHP app to calculate airline miles from flight information. After building this project, what are the possible reasons we'd want to change the program after it's built? Well, maybe we want to change the algorithm for generating the points, or maybe the UI for displaying the calculation. These are fundamentally our "reasons to change" and therefore we consider them to be responsibilities under the SRP (Single Responsibility Principle).

Every module or class should only be responsible of one piece of functionality and it should fully encapsulate that responsibility. Within the context of the SRP we consider a responsibility to be "a reason to change". By combining responsibilities we can cause some nasty issues, such as tight-coupling and making code-reuse harder.

Let's assume a project manager has given us an airline miles calculator app to refactor, and it doesn't match this principle. Let's refactor it so it does. The code have been given contains a single `Miles` class which has both the HTML that contains the User Interface and the business logic that runs the points calculation:

```php
1   <?php
2
3   class Miles
4   {
5       public function render(): string
6       {
7           if (isset($_POST['distance'])) {
8               return $this->getMiles();
9           }
10
11          return $this->getForm();
12      }
13
14      public function calculateMiles(int $distance, bool $businessClass, bool $fly\
15  ingClubMember): int
16      {
17          $multiplier = 1;
18
19          if ($businessClass === true) {
20              $multiplier *= 2;
21          }
22
23          if ($flyingClubMember === true) {
24              $multiplier *= 2;
25          }
26
27          return $distance * $multiplier;
28      }
29
30      private function getMiles(): string
31      {
32          $miles = $this->calculateMiles(
33              $_POST['distance'],
34              isset($_POST['businessclass']),
35              isset($_POST['flyingclubmember'])
36          );
37
38          return $this->loadPage('<p>You have: <b>' . $miles . ' miles</b>.</p>');
39      }
40
41      private function getForm(): string
42      {
```

```
43          return $this->loadPage('
44 <form action="" method="POST">
45   Distance:
46   <input type="number" name="distance" min="0" step="1" />
47   <br>
48   Business Class Flyer:
49   <input type="checkbox" name="businessclass"><br>
50   Flying Club Member:
51   <input type="checkbox" name="flyingclubmember">
52   <br><br>
53   <input type="submit" value="Submit">
54 </form>
55          ');
56      }
57
58      private function loadPage(string $html): string
59      {
60          return '
61 <!DOCTYPE html>
62 <html>
63   <body>
64     ' . $html . '
65   </body>
66 </html>
67          ';
68      }
69 }
```

Our business logic is horribly intertwined with HTML, the Miles class conjoins our calculator logic with the code that renders the web page meaning the class is responsible for both the presentation and calculation of reward miles. By separating presentation from our business logic we can better prevent duplicate code and ensure our class supplies with the Single Responsibility Principle.

We can utilise this class with the following index.php file:

```
1 <?php
2
3 require_once('Miles.php');
4
5 $calculator = new Miles();
6 echo $calculator->render();
```

This makes code reuse more difficult, a developer might not want to pull in a bloated class into another part of the application just to do a simple points calculation. When a class does more and more, as developers are reluctant to add classes to a project, this leads to an Anti-Pattern known as the "God Class". An irrational fear of adding classes to a project converges to there being one "God Class" which has multiple responsibilities throughout the application. Functions with different responsibilities become tightly bound to each other, and the code becomes a ball of mud.

Now let's refactor this `Miles` class so we have a `MilesCalculator` class containing the business logic and a `MilesUI` class containing the GUI. Our UI class looks like this:

```php
<?php

class MilesUI
{
    private $calculator;

    public function __construct(Calculator $calculator)
    {
        $this->calculator = $calculator;
    }

    public function render(): string
    {
        if (isset($_POST['distance'])) {
            return $this->getMiles();
        }

        return $this->getForm();
    }

    private function getMiles(): string
    {
        $miles = $this->calculator->calculate(
            $_POST['distance'],
            isset($_POST['businessclass']),
            isset($_POST['flyingclubmember'])
        );

        return $this->loadPage('<p>You have: <b>' . $miles . ' miles</b>.</p>');
    }

    private function getForm(): string
    {
        return $this->loadPage('
<form action="" method="POST">
```

```
36    Distance:
37    <input type="number" name="distance" min="0" step="1" />
38    <br>
39    Business Class Flyer:
40    <input type="checkbox" name="businessclass"><br>
41    Flying Club Member:
42    <input type="checkbox" name="flyingclubmember">
43    <br><br>
44    <input type="submit" value="Submit">
45  </form>
46          ');
47      }
48
49      private function loadPage(string $html): string
50      {
51          return '
52  <!DOCTYPE html>
53  <html>
54    <body>
55      ' . $html . '
56    </body>
57  </html>
58          ';
59      }
60  }
```

Note that our UI class contains some HTML, this is acceptable when well managed - but it sometimes can be easier to use a template engine to manage HTML, one such engine is Twig[3]. A more optimal solution is simply to have PHP serve an API which a Javascript framework like React or Vue.js can consume. Regardless of how you chose to do it, it's vital the UI class is separate from your business logic, in this example we're ensuring that the UI is managed by a separate class.

When instantiating this UI class, we inject a `Calculator` interface - this interface looks like this:

---

[3]http://twig.sensiolabs.org/

```php
1   <?php
2
3   interface Calculator
4   {
5       public function calculate(int $distance, bool $businessClass, bool $flyingCl\
6   ubMember): int;
7   }
```

This interface is then implemented in our `MilesCalculator` class, this is our concrete implementation of our `Calculator` interface that we can use with our `MilesUI` class:

```php
1   <?php
2
3   class MilesCalculator implements Calculator
4   {
5       public function calculate(int $distance, bool $businessClass, bool $flyingCl\
6   ubMember): int
7       {
8           $multiplier = $this->getMultiplier($businessClass, $flyingClubMember);
9
10          return $distance * $multiplier;
11      }
12
13      private function getMultiplier(bool $businessClass, bool $flyingClubMember):\
14  int
15      {
16          $multiplier = 1;
17
18          if ($businessClass === true) {
19              $multiplier *= 2;
20          }
21
22          if ($flyingClubMember === true) {
23              $multiplier *= 2;
24          }
25
26          return $multiplier;
27      }
28  }
```

Our index.php file looks much the same as it did earlier, except we inject an instance of `MilesCal-culator` into `MilesUI`:

```
 1  <?php
 2
 3  require_once('MilesUI.php');
 4  require_once('Calculator.php');
 5  require_once('MilesCalculator.php');
 6
 7  $calculator = new MilesCalculator();
 8
 9  $ui = new MilesUI($calculator);
10  echo $ui->render();
```

Notice that so far in this book, we've been testing code snippets by running them from the terminal? In this example let's do things slightly differently and use the in-built development server in PHP by running this command from the terminal:

```
 1  php -S localhost:8000
```

The server will then spin into action and we can access webpage at http://localhost:8000:

Let's fill out the form with a 3000 mile business class flight with Flying Club membership:

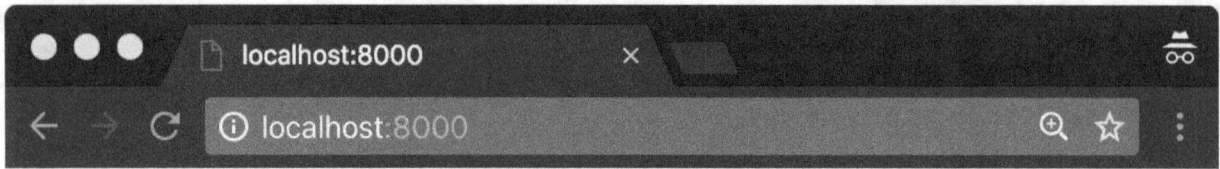

Distance: 3000

Business Class Flyer:

Flying Club Member: ✔

With the form filled out, we should then get a result of 12000 reward miles:

You have: **12000 miles**.

The Single Responsibility Principle can be violated in many other ways; if we had a system for employee data with the underlying data being stored in JSON, we should avoid creating a class which simultaneously contains business logic for the employee data whilst also having the class hold the logic for dealing with the persistence layer (storing and managing the JSON in the file system).

The Single Responsibility Principle is one of the most core principles to writing Object-Oriented code and it should be something you start to do naturally by considering the axis for change for each class.

Open/Closed Principle

The Open/Closed Principle states "software entities (classes, modules, functions, etc.) should be open for extension, but closed for modification".

Simply, this means that we should be able to extended a given piece of software without needing to modify it's source code. In the context of OOP, this means we should be able to extend a classes behaviour without needing to modifying it. This fundamentally comes down to two core attributes:

- "Open for Extension" - we can make the class behave in new ways as the requirements for what the class needs to do evolves
- "Closed for Modification" - you cannot change the source code of the class itself, it is considered inviolable

This principle is said to be originally coined by the French software engineer, Bertrand Meyer, in his 1988 book *Object Oriented Software Construction*.

Whilst these principles may seem at odds with each other, they aren't. Let me demonstrate how we can extend a class using the Object Decorator Pattern. Imagine our MilesCalculator class from earlier needs to be extended for a new MilesPlus program. With a MilesPlus credit card, Flying Club members in Business class get a 1500 mile bonus for each flight - if these criteria aren't met the standard calculator applies.

Our Calculator interface is the same as before:

```php
<?php

interface Calculator
{
    public function calculate(int $distance, bool $businessClass, bool $flyingCl\
ubMember): int;
}
```

The same goes for our MilesCalculator class from before:

```php
1   <?php
2
3   class MilesCalculator implements Calculator
4   {
5       public function calculate(int $distance, bool $businessClass, bool $flyingCl\
6   ubMember): int
7       {
8           $multiplier = $this->getMultiplier($businessClass, $flyingClubMember);
9
10          return $distance * $multiplier;
11      }
12
13      private function getMultiplier(bool $businessClass, bool $flyingClubMember):\
14   int
15      {
16          $multiplier = 1;
17
18          if ($businessClass === true) {
19              $multiplier *= 2;
20          }
21
22          if ($flyingClubMember === true) {
23              $multiplier *= 2;
24          }
25
26          return $multiplier;
27      }
28  }
```

Our MilesPlusCalculator is where things start to get interesting, we are treating this like the MilesCalculator by implementing the Calculator interface:

```php
1   <?php
2
3   class MilesPlusCalculator implements Calculator
4   {
5       private $milesCalculator;
6
7       public function __construct()
8       {
9           $this->milesCalculator = new MilesCalculator();
10      }
```

```
11
12      public function calculate(int $distance, bool $businessClass, bool $flyingCl\
13  ubMember): int
14      {
15          $miles = $this->milesCalculator->calculate($distance, $businessClass, $f\
16  lyingClubMember);
17
18          if ($businessClass === true && $flyingClubMember === true) {
19              $miles += 1500;
20          }
21
22          return $miles;
23      }
24  }
```

When the new class is instantiated, it creates a private instance of the MilesCalculator class and stores it in $milesCalculator for when it needs it. When the calculation actually takes place, the calculate() method uses the $milesCalculator instance to find what the old value should be then if the criteria for the bonus miles are met - the method adds them too.

Liscov Substitution Principle

In it's simplified form: "Functions that use pointers or references to base classes must be able to use objects of derived classes without knowing it".

Fundamentally this principle means that any class should be substitutable for it's base class or interface; if we have an interface called Shape and a class called Square, we should be able to replace any instance of Square with another object that meets the Shape interface and it should work as normal. This definition of a subtype relation was named after Barbara Liskov in a 1987 conference keynote address titled *Data abstraction and hierarchy.*

Suppose we have an abstract class called Staff (this could just as easily be an interface or a normal class), to this we're going to add two concrete implementations of this in Manager and Executive:

```php
1   <?php
2
3   abstract class Staff
4   {
5       protected $baseSalary;
6       private $paid;
7
8       public function __construct(double $baseSalary)
9       {
10          $this->baseSalary = $baseSalary;
11      }
12
13      public abstract function getWeeklyHours(): double;
14
15      public abstract function getSalary(): double;
16
17      public function pay(double $bonus): bool
18      {
19          $this->paid += $this->getSalary() + $bonus;
20
21          return true;
22      }
23  }
```

The first concrete implementation we'll build will be Executive:

```php
1   <?php
2
3   class Executive extends Staff
4   {
5       public function getWeeklyHours(): double
6       {
7           return 37.5;
8       }
9
10      public function getSalary(): double
11      {
12          return $this->baseSalary;
13      }
14  }
```

Similarly, we can build another concrete implementation called Manager:

```php
1   <?php
2
3   class Manager extends Staff
4   {
5       public function getWeeklyHours(): double
6       {
7           return 40;
8       }
9
10      public function getSalary(): double
11      {
12          return $this->baseSalary * 1.2;
13      }
14  }
```

However; now suppose we want to add an UnpaidIntern class - we will quickly find that the pay() would end up needing to be overwritten to do absolutely nothing:

```php
1   <?php
2
3   class UnpaidIntern
4   {
5       public function getWeeklyHours(): double
6       {
7           return 35;
8       }
9
10      public function getSalary(): double
11      {
12          return 0;
13      }
14
15      public function pay(double $bonus): bool
16      {
17          return false;
18      }
19  }
```

Our UnpaidIntern class is extending our Staff class but changing the behaviour of the underlying Staff abstract method so it breeches this principle. Suppose we then add an additional method to our UnpaidIntern class, this poses another breech of the principle:

```
1   public function makeCoffee(): bool
2   {
3       return true;
4   }
```

As we have added a public method which doesn't exist in the original interface, we introduce a situation whereby instances of the UnpaidIntern class cannot be substituted for other instances of the Staff abstract class.

Another more hypothetical example that has been coined before is the example of a Rectangle class which mandates a setWidth() and a setHeight() method. When we extend this class to a Square class mandating both a setWidth() and a setHeight() method no longer makes sense. You change one property, and the other must change - all sides must be equal in a square. It is a mathematical impossibility to independently change the $width and the $height property when we talk about a square. Therefore the Square inheriting a Rectangle class fails the Liskov Substitution Test as you cannot ensure they're both the same without having a check after the property has been changed to make sure both the $width and the $height property are the same.

Interface Segregation Principle

The Interface Segregation Principle states that no client should be forced to depend on methods it does not use.

This principle essentially outlines that we should favour small, specific interfaces over large bloated ones. All classes should only have to implement the methods they need - this helps keep our system decoupled. I'll demonstrate this with a simple example of a CardReader interface:

```
1   <?php
2
3   interface BadCardReader
4   {
5       public function __construct(string $cardNumber, string $expiry, string $pin);
6
7       public function withdraw(double $amount): bool;
8
9       public function deposit(double $amount): bool;
10  }
```

In order for a ATM to implement this interface, it has to have a deposit() method, even if it might only be used for withdrawing money from accounts with the withdraw() method. Similarly a DepositKiosk class might only need the deposit() method but it has to contain the withdraw() method.

Let's simplify the interface down so that the new CardReader interface contains the constructor and a method which generates the security auth tokens required to check balances, perform withdrawals and add deposits. We can leave the logic which actually does that behaviour in a separate class which satisfies a separate interface. In short we are closely aligning our CardReader interface to a single responsibility and in doing so we ensure that classes implementing it don't have to depend on methods they don't use:

```php
1  <?php
2
3  interface CardReader
4  {
5      public function __construct(string $cardNumber, string $expiry, string $auth\
6  Code);
7
8      public function getAuthCode(): double;
9  }
```

We can then build an interface for CashDispenser which our ATM class will later be able to use:

```php
1  <?php
2
3  interface CashDispenser
4  {
5      public function __construct(CardReader $reader);
6
7      public function withdraw(double $amount): bool;
8  }
```

By injecting an instance of CardReader into the CashDispenser we are able to use the getAuthCode() method from the CashDispenser() method. In a similar light, we are are also able to build an interface for our DepositKiosk using the CashDepository interface:

```php
1  <?php
2
3  interface CashDepository
4  {
5      public function __construct(CardReader $reader);
6
7      public function deposit(double $amount): bool;
8  }
```

We now have two specific interfaces, meaning our CashDispenser interface isn't bloated and ensuring our classes are decoupled from each other. Interface Bloat is an anti-pattern by which interfaces become so large that code which has different responsibilities becomes tied together in one interface. By abiding by the Interface Segregation Principle we help ensure Interface Bloat is prevented and our code remains decoupled well.

Dependency-Inversion Principle

The Dependency-Inversion Principle is stated in two parts:

- High-level modules should not depend on low-level modules. Both should depend on abstractions.
- Abstractions should not depend on details. Details should depend on abstractions.

When developing software it is common for us to have high-level classes which need to depend on low-level classes. We can have a Users class which depends upon a Database class. In Chapter 3 we actually looked at an example of using a class to read from a JSON file, I'll use a truncated versioned of that example here. We start with a JSON file that looks like this:

```
1   [
2     {
3       "text": "junade.com",
4       "type": "link"
5     },
6     {
7       "text": "It's raining today.",
8       "type": "text"
9     },
10    {
11      "text": "icyapril.com",
12      "type": "link"
13    },
14    {
15      "text": "Hello world!",
16      "type": "text"
17    }
18  ]
```

Accordingly we have a simple class to read the JSON file (our low-level module):

```php
1    <?php
2
3    class JSON
4    {
5        private $data;
6
7        public function __construct(string $file)
8        {
9            $this->processFile($file);
10       }
11
12       private function processFile(string $file)
13       {
14           $contents     = file_get_contents($file);
15           $array        = json_decode($contents);
16           $arrayReverse = array_reverse($array);
17           $this->data   = $arrayReverse;
18       }
19
20       public function getData(): array
21       {
22           return $this->data;
23       }
24
25       public function getDataByType(string $type): array
26       {
27           $result = [];
28           $data   = $this->getData();
29
30           foreach ($data as $entry) {
31               if ($entry->type === $type) {
32                   array_push($result, $entry);
33               }
34           }
35
36           return $result;
37       }
38   }
```

This low-level module is in turn consumed by our high-level module (our Link class):

```php
1   <?php
2
3   class Link
4   {
5       private $data;
6
7       public function __construct(JSON $data)
8       {
9           $this->data = $data;
10      }
11
12      public function getContent(): Generator
13      {
14          $links = $this->data->getDataByType('link');
15
16          foreach ($links as $link) {
17              yield $link->text;
18          }
19      }
20  }
```

There is, however a fairly major issue in this Link class - what if we want to read from an XML file instead of a JSON file? Our current Link class makes explicitly clear that we are injecting a concrete JSON class instead of a generic File interface. In order to comply with the Dependency-Inversion Principle we need to build a File interface for our JSON file:

```php
1   <?php
2
3   interface File
4   {
5       public function __construct(string $file);
6
7       public function getData(): array;
8
9       public function getDataByType(string $type): array;
10  }
```

Let's go ahead and amend our JSON class to implement this:

```
1  <?php
2
3  class JSON implements File
4  ...
```

With this in place our constructor for our `Link` class can be refactored so it type hints for the `File` interface instead of the concrete `JSON` class.

```
1  public function __construct(File $data)
```

Finally, our `index.php` file demonstrates how this can all be put together:

```
1   <?php
2
3   require_once('File.php');
4   require_once('JSON.php');
5   require_once('Link.php');
6
7   $data = new JSON('data.json');
8   $link = new Link($data);
9
10  foreach ($link->getContent() as $content) {
11      echo $content. "\n";
12  }
```

The script outputs the links we desired; the added benefit is now that should we want to replace our low-level `JSON` class, we can do that so long as the `File` interface is met:

```
[junades-mbp:Dependency-InversionPrinciple junade$ php index.php
[icyapril.com
junade.com
junades-mbp:Dependency-InversionPrinciple junade$ ▯
```

Conclusion

In this chapter we've discussed the SOLID Design Principles and how they can help make sure you write great code; ensuring your code is decoupled, extendable and will be easy to test later down the road. There are some things here which go unsaid; you still need to ensure your code is descriptively named and that you aren't repeating code.

In the next chapter we'll start to discuss Design Patterns which provide effective but reusable solutions to common programming problems.

An Introduction to Design Patterns

The concept of software design patterns is routed in Christopher Alexanders 1977 book, *A Pattern Language*. Alexander is not a software engineer but a building architect - he proposed that a Pattern Language could be used for architecting and improving their own communities.

In Christopher Alexander's own words:

> "The elements of this language are entities called patterns. Each pattern describes a problem that occurs over and over again in our environment, and then describes the core of the solution to that problem, in such a way that you can use this solution a million times over, without ever doing it the same way twice."

One example of such a Pattern 12 in the book is known as the Community of 7000:

> "Individuals have no effective voice in any community of more than 5,000-10,000 persons."

From architecture we move onto the *Gang of Four*, the name coined for the authors of *Design Patterns: Elements of Reusable Object-Oriented Software*. The book they produced became one of the most highly influential books in Object-Oriented Programming and Software Engineering in general. The first chapter discusses Object-Oriented Programming principles based on the authors experience, with the second chapter discusses a case-study involving the step-by-step process of designing a document editor. In total the book describes 23 software design patterns in three separate categories: Creational Design Patterns, Structural Design Patterns and Behavioural Design Patterns.

When developing software we'll often find that we encounter recurring problems that Design Patterns can help us solve in a consistent and well-designed way. I have written a separate (and far more lengthy) book on PHP Design Patterns and we have already touched on some fundamental patterns in other chapters within this book - but in this chapter I'd like to cover some of the most useful *Gang-of-Four* Design Patterns to keep in your inventory.

Throughout this book we've already seen a number of patterns as they've emerged through the course of software development; in the previous chapter on SOLID Principles we discussed the "Open/Closed Principle" and how the Decorator Pattern pattern can help us. The Gang of Four categorised this as a Structural Design Pattern.

In our Advanced Concepts chapter, we also discussed how Generators can be use to easily create Iterators - the Gang of Four included implementing Iterators as a Behavioral pattern.

Let's now cover some new ones.

Design Pattern Principles

In the last chapter we covered SOLID Design Principles, and how they can help us write better code. When reading through the Design Patterns described in this chapter please ensure you keep these principles in mind. Additionally, be sure to keep the following additional principles in mind:

- KISS Principle
- DRY Principle

KISS stands for "Keep it Simple, Stupid", fundamentally this means that you should keep your software design as concise and simple as possible to perform the task at hand. Adding unnecessary abstraction or complexity can be kept for later when it is needed. In the final chapter of this book we'll discuss refactoring and how the design of existing code can be adapted to new functionality. Adding additional complexity when it's not needed will likely mean it's never used, adds no value to the customer and makes the codebase unnecessarily complicated. It is right that our code is written to be resilient to the forces of change and we'll discuss how this can be done over the next two chapters.

DRY stands for "Don't Repeat Yourself" and it simply means that you shouldn't duplicate code within the codebase. Modification of a single element of a codebase should not require changes in unrelated parts of the codebase.

Creational Design Patterns

Creational Design Patterns deal with object creation. Using constructors alone to create objects can lead to design problems or add unnecessary complexity. By combining objects creatively together, we are able to abstract object creation away from our software.

Factory

Suppose are creating a Taxi app - the Taxi company serves 2 different cars; a BMW 3 Series (medium-sized) and a BMW 7 Series (luxury). If the user selects the Luxury mode they will get a 7 Series, else they will get a BMW 3 Series. Where do we put the logic which constructs returns the class of the correct class? This is where factories come into play, they are classes which contain the logic to create and return objects according to the specifications we want.

Factories in real-life create new objects according to a given specification and return them to us. That's exactly what our pattern here does.

Our abstraction for our cars will be our Car interface that contains a drive() method:

```php
1  <?php
2
3  interface Car
4  {
5      public function drive(): string;
6  }
```

Our first implementation for our Three Series looks like this:

```php
1  <?php
2
3  class BMWThreeSeries implements Car
4  {
5      public function drive(): string
6      {
7          return "Vroum Vroum!";
8      }
9  }
```

Similarly we can create one for our Seven Series using the same interface:

```php
1  <?php
2
3  class BMWSevenSeries implements Car
4  {
5      public function drive(): string
6      {
7          return "The luxury!";
8      }
9  }
```

The logic of determining which class to use can be designated to a Factory class which looks something like this:

```php
1   <?php
2
3   class CarFactory
4   {
5       public static function getCar(bool $luxury): Car {
6           if ($luxury === true) {
7               return new BMWSevenSeries();
8           }
9
10          return new BMWThreeSeries();
11      }
12  }
```

Regardless of how complicated the logic of deciding between which class to use is, we can have a class which does that behaviour and can be consumed easily by our application:

```php
1   $car = CarFactory::getCar(false);
2   echo $car->drive();
```

That's all their is to it! This is an incredibly simple pattern whereby we use one class to construct and return another. The above example would return a medium size car with the output being Vroum Vroum!

Abstract Factory

The Taxi firm decides to expand their offering to include Limobikes (a kinda taxi motorbike service, and yes, it is a real service that you can use in London). There needs to be a separate factory for Limobike that creates two different types of motorcycle Yamaha Motor (medium-sized) and BMW Motorrad (luxury).

In order to refactor our existing Factory to be abstracted we must first create a VehicleFactory for us to use:

```php
1   <?php
2
3   interface VehicleFactory
4   {
5       public static function getVehicle(bool $luxury): Vehicle;
6   }
```

We can then refactor our CarFactory class to use this interface:

```php
1   <?php
2
3   class CarFactory implements VehicleFactory
4   {
5       public static function getVehicle(bool $luxury): Vehicle {
6           if ($luxury === true) {
7               return new BMWSevenSeries();
8           }
9
10          return new BMWThreeSeries();
11      }
12  }
```

Similarly, we create a MotorbikeFactory which works of the same VehicleFactory interface:

```php
1   <?php
2
3   class MotorbikeFactory implements VehicleFactory
4   {
5       public static function getVehicle(bool $luxury): Vehicle
6       {
7           if ($luxury === true) {
8               return new BMWMotorrad();
9           }
10
11          return new YamahaMotor();
12      }
13
14  }
```

This pattern can seem a little daunting, especially for those learning it from the old textbooks - but in actually all we're doing is building multiple factories from a common interface, for each type of object we're creating.

In short; we are creating a factory that abstracts away other factories. Factory-ception!

Builder Pattern

Sometimes our class constructors can get incredibly complicated by adding more and more variables. Imagine how many different constructor variables could go into instantiating a Pizza class (extra cheese, ingredients, size, sauce, etc).

Let's take an example class:

```php
1   <?php
2
3   class Pizza
4   {
5       private $recipe;
6       private $extraCheese;
7       private $size;
8       private $sauce;
9
10
11      public function __construct(string $recipe, bool $extraCheese, int $size, st\
12  ring $sauce)
13      {
14          $this->recipe = $recipe;
15          $this->extraCheese = $extraCheese;
16          $this->size = $size;
17          $this->sauce = $sauce;
18      }
19
20      public function getLabel(): string
21      {
22          $cheese = $this->extraCheese ? " (with extra cheese) " : "";
23
24          return $this->recipe . $cheese . " pizza with " . $this->sauce . " sauce\
25  . Diameter (inches): " . $this->size;
26      }
27  }
```

Our constructor is very long and confusing (and could easily be more so), let's abstract away our constructor from the class itself. In order to do this, let's create a simple ""Builder" class to store the values which were previously in our constructor:

```php
1   <?php
2
3   class PizzaBuilder
4   {
5       private $recipe;
6       private $extraCheese;
7       private $size;
8       private $sauce;
9
10      public function __construct(string $recipe)
```

```
11          {
12              $this->recipe = $recipe;
13              $this->extraCheese = false;
14              $this->size = 9;
15              $this->sauce = "tomato";
16          }
17
18          public function addCheese()
19          {
20              $this->extraCheese = true;
21          }
22
23          public function setSize(int $size)
24          {
25              $this->size = $size;
26          }
27
28          public function setSauce(string $sauce)
29          {
30              $this->sauce = $sauce;
31          }
32
33          public function __get($name)
34          {
35              return $this->$name;
36          }
37      }
```

Our Pizza class can then be modified to use the constructor arguments from the PizzaBuilder
instance:

```
1   <?php
2
3   class Pizza
4   {
5       private $recipe;
6       private $extraCheese;
7       private $size;
8       private $sauce;
9
10      public function __construct(PizzaBuilder $builder)
11          {
```

```
12          $this->recipe = $builder->recipe;
13          $this->extraCheese = $builder->extraCheese;
14          $this->size = $builder->size;
15          $this->sauce = $builder->sauce;
16      }
17
18      public function getLabel(): string
19      {
20          $cheese = $this->extraCheese ? " (with extra cheese) " : "";
21
22          return $this->recipe . $cheese . " pizza with " . $this->sauce . " sauce\
23  . Diameter (inches): " . $this->size;
24      }
25  }
```

This can then be put together as follows:

```
1   $builder = new PizzaBuilder('Margarita');
2   $builder->addCheese();
3   $builder->setSize(9);
4   $builder->setSauce('BBQ');
5
6   $pizza = new Pizza($builder);
7   echo $pizza->getLabel();
```

It's as simple as that; we've reduced the amount of variables going into our constructor whilst still allowing type hinting (if we passed in an array instead an object of type PizzaBuilder we'd have no such type hinting).

Some developers like to return the instance after each function executes, like this:

```
1   ...
2   public function addCheese(): PizzaBuilder
3   {
4       $this->extraCheese = true;
5
6       return $this;
7   }
8
9   public function setSize(int $size): PizzaBuilder
10  {
11      $this->size = $size;
```

```
12
13      return $this;
14  }
15  ...
```

This allows for a more clean way to put together Builders:

```
1  $builder = (new PizzaBuilder('Margarita'))
2                      ->addCheese()
3                      ->setSauce('BBQ');
```

Where should validation be done with the Builder pattern? Well the Builder already has the responsibility of aggregating data for the constructor, does making it responsible for validation violate the Single Responsibility Principle? Well, the responsibility of a Builder is to aggregate *valid* data for the construction of another object. The single "Reason to Change" is the properties that the Builder is aggregating, the validity of the properties is intrinsic to them being valid properties - so therefore doesn't represent an additional "Reason to Change".

In short; it is perfectly valid for the Builder to check if the properties are valid at a high-level. It would therefore be okay to put this inside our PizzaBuilder class:

```
1   ...
2   public function setSize(int $size)
3   {
4       if ($size < 4) {
5           throw new Exception('Pizza too small!');
6       }
7
8       $this->size = $size;
9   }
10  ...
```

That's all there is to the Builder pattern, this pattern provides an intuitive way to decouple constructor variables when instantiating an object, allowing for re-use and clearer use of such variables.

Structural Design Patterns

Structural Design Patterns affect how we structure code within a classes. They allow us to create simple relationships between different pieces of business logic.

Composite Pattern

Sometimes we have to deal with trees of data. Consider different types of music; we can have individual Songs and we can have Albums formed of Songs. When we iterate through Playlists, these can either contain Albums or individual Songs, but we want all the resulting Songs to be treated the same.

Let's create a simple interface which both our Album and Song classes implement, Music:

```php
1   <?php
2
3   interface Music
4   {
5       public function play(): string;
6   }
```

Our Song class is a very simple implementation of this:

```php
1   <?php
2
3   class Song implements Music
4   {
5       private $name;
6
7       public function __construct(string $name)
8       {
9           $this->name = $name;
10      }
11
12      public function play(): string
13      {
14          return "Playing song: ".$this->name;
15      }
16  }
```

Our Album class is a more complicated implementation of our Music class. It had has an addSong() method to add individual Song objects:

```php
1   <?php
2
3   class Album implements Music
4   {
5       private $name;
6       private $songs = array();
7
8       public function __construct(string $name)
9       {
10          $this->name = $name;
11      }
12
13      public function addSong(Music $song)
14      {
15          array_push($this->songs, $song);
16      }
17
18      public function play(): string
19      {
20          $songNames = array();
21
22          foreach ($this->songs as $song) {
23              array_push($songNames, $song->play());
24          }
25
26          $songList = implode("", $songNames);
27
28          return "Playing album: " . $this->name . "\n" . $songList . "\n";
29      }
30  }
```

Let's demonstrate how these classes fit together in an index.php, we can instantiate some instances of our Song class and an instance of an Album class. Instances of Song can be grouped together in instances of Album, either songs or albums can be both played using the same play() method:

```php
1   <?php
2
3   require_once('Music.php');
4   require_once('Song.php');
5   require_once('Album.php');
6
7   $lostInStereo = new Song('Lost in Stereo');
8   $guts = new Song('Guts');
9   $helloBrooklyn = new Song('Hello, Brooklyn');
10  $poison = new Song('Poison');
11
12  $fences = new Song("Fences");
13
14  $album = new Album('Nothing Personal');
15  $album->addSong($lostInStereo);
16  $album->addSong($guts);
17  $album->addSong($helloBrooklyn);
18
19
20  echo $album->play();
21  echo $fences->play();
```

We can run this script by running php index.php and we get an output like this:

```
1   Playing album: Nothing Personal
2   Playing song: Lost in Stereo
3   Playing song: Guts
4   Playing song: Hello, Brooklyn
5
6   Playing song: Fences
```

This pattern allows us to treat a group of objects like the object itself in an easy and unified manor.

Another quick fact, notice that in our Album class we declare the addSong function as public function addSong(Music $song). We are type hinting our song as an instance of Music instead of Song, this means that in theory - we are able to create albums of other albums. This implementation of this pattern allows us to create branches which lead to other branches.

Branches on a tree can be of varying length, the point of this pattern is that the leaves at the end of branch are treated the same regardless of branch length.

Adapter Pattern

Think back to the Decorators we covered in the last chapter, we could add features to an existing class by encapsulating it an other. Adapters encapsulate another class so that interface can match a different interface.

A British plug matches a British plug interface; however this isn't much use when we're in the US. We instead need a US plug adapter to match a US plug interface. The Adapter Pattern works much like this by having an abstraction layer to fit one plug into a different interface.

Imagine we have a Comment class - however our existing Comment class must be ported to work in the context of a new Forum app. As such we need to map our Comment class onto the following Reply interface:

```php
<?php

interface Reply
{
    public function __construct(string $threadID, string $body, int $timestamp);

    public function addLike();

    public function getBody(): string;

    public function getTimestamp(): int;

    public function getLikes(): int;
}
```

Our original Comment class looks like this:

```php
<?php

class Comment
{
    private $thread;
    private $body;
    private $time;
    private $likes;

    public function __construct(string $body, int $time, string $thread)
    {
        $this->thread = $thread;
```

```
13            $this->body = $body;
14            $this->time = $time;
15            $this->likes = 0;
16        }
17
18        public function addLike()
19        {
20            $this->likes++;
21        }
22
23        public function showBody(): string
24        {
25            return $this->body;
26        }
27
28        public function showTime(): int
29        {
30            return $this->time;
31        }
32
33        public function countLikes(): int
34        {
35            return $this->likes;
36        }
37    }
```

In order to map our Comment class onto the Reply interface, I've created a CommentAdapter class which encapsulates our Comment class.

```
1    <?php
2
3    class CommentAdapter implements Reply
4    {
5        private $comment;
6
7        public function __construct(string $threadID, string $body, int $timestamp)
8        {
9            $this->comment = new Comment($body, $timestamp, $threadID);
10        }
11
12        public function addLike()
13        {
```

```
14          return $this->comment->addLike();
15      }
16
17      public function getBody(): string
18      {
19          return $this->comment->showBody();
20      }
21
22      public function getTimestamp(): int
23      {
24          return $this->comment->showTime();
25      }
26
27      public function getLikes(): int
28      {
29          return $this->comment->countLikes();
30      }
31
32  }
```

This is a simple pattern that allows us to map a class of one interface onto another, we effectively are able to continue to use a common interface without needing to but caveats in our code. This is a pattern which becomes vital when reusing code or dealing with old classes.

Behavioural Design Patterns

Behavioural Design Patterns apply flexibility to how objects can intercommunicate; there are times when objects need to be able to update each other, or align objects in order when processing data. This is where Behavioural patterns can help increase flexibility of objects communicating together.

Chain-of-Responsibility Pattern

Sometimes part of your business logic is formed of a chain of links. Imagine at work an executive has the ability to purchase something up to $1000, their manager can purchase up to $10,000 and their Head of Department can purchase up to $100,000. If a higher purchase is required the CEOs approval is required. If we were to purchase something the request would go first to the executive and they'd purchase if they could, if not they'd escalate to their manager. Their manager would also check if they could purchase and if not they'd escalate again - this escalation would go all the way up to the CEO who would purchase (or the algorithm would fail).

Let's take a look at how this looks in code, first I'm going to create a simple interface for our Purchasers to use:

```php
1   <?php
2
3   interface Purchaser
4   {
5       public function setNextPurchaser(Purchaser $nextPurchaser);
6
7       public function buy(float $price): bool;
8   }
```

Our Executive example class can then implement this interface:

```php
1   <?php
2
3   class Executive implements Purchaser
4   {
5       private $nextPurchaser;
6
7       public function setNextPurchaser(Purchaser $nextPurchaser)
8       {
9           $this->nextPurchaser = $nextPurchaser;
10      }
11
12      public function buy(float $price): bool
13      {
14          if ($price <= 1000) {
15              echo "Executive purchased";
16              return true;
17          }
18
19          if (isset($this->nextPurchaser)) {
20              return $this->nextPurchaser->buy($price);
21          }
22
23          echo "Could not purchase";
24          return false;
25      }
26  }
```

This class contains a setNextPurchaser() method which allows another Purchaser to be defined for the buy() method to use if it can't handle the data itself. I've then created near-identical other classes for Manager, HeadOfDepartment and CEO, just with different purchase limit. In reality, your different Purchaser classes could contain vastly different logic (if they don't you should consider abstracting those methods away, such as to an abstract class). For the sake of an example, here's the Manager class:

```php
<?php

class Manager implements Purchaser
{
    private $nextPurchaser;

    public function setNextPurchaser(Purchaser $nextPurchaser)
    {
        $this->nextPurchaser = $nextPurchaser;
    }

    public function buy(float $price): bool
    {
        if ($price <= 10000) {
            echo "Manager purchased";
            return true;
        }

        if (isset($this->nextPurchaser)) {
            return $this->nextPurchaser->buy($price);
        }

        echo "Could not purchase";
        return false;
    }
}
```

The index.php file contains a very simple example of how this is used to create a chain of classes:

```php
<?php

require_once('Purchaser.php');
require_once('Executive.php');
require_once('Manager.php');
require_once('HeadOfDepartment.php');
require_once('CEO.php');

$developer = new Executive();
$engineeringManager = new Manager();
```

```
11  $headOfEngineering = new HeadOfDepartment();
12  $ceo = new CEO();
13
14  $developer->setNextPurchaser($engineeringManager);
15  $engineeringManager->setNextPurchaser($headOfEngineering);
16  $headOfEngineering->setNextPurchaser($ceo);
17
18  $developer->buy(500);
19  echo "\n";
20  $developer->buy(5000);
21  echo "\n";
22  $developer->buy(50000);
23  echo "\n";
24  $developer->buy(500000);
25  echo "\n";
```

When we run this example, we can see the chain of responsibility, for a price of 500 the `Executive` can purchase, for 5000 the `Manager` can purchase, etc - however regardless of who is purchasing we can still enter through a common object and the logic will find the next responsible object in the chain:

```
1  Executive purchased
2  Manager purchased
3  Executive purchased
4  CEO purchased
```

The Chain-of-Responsibility pattern allows us to split processing logic into a chain of objects; the object will handle what it can, and the other cases will be passed up the chain to a different object that can process the data instead. There are many use cases for this simple but intuitive pattern, from authentication to data processing.

Observer Pattern

There are cases where we have an object with some dependent objects. By implementing the Observer pattern, the `Subject` object is updated, the `Observer` classes will be updated automatically.

The PHP default Standard Package Library contains two interfaces which allow us to effectively implement this pattern incredibly easily, `SplObserver` and `SplSubject`.

The `SplObserver` interface contains a simple update method for `SplSubject` classes to run in order to update observers:

```
1  SplObserver {
2    /* Methods */
3    abstract public void update ( SplSubject $subject )
4  }
```

The SplSubject interface contains other methods in order to allow for SplObserver classes to be attached to it so they can monitor it for changes:

```
1  SplSubject {
2    /* Methods */
3    abstract public void attach ( SplObserver $observer )
4    abstract public void detach ( SplObserver $observer )
5    abstract public void notify ( void )
6  }
```

Let's assume we're building an RSS reader app, we have users following a feed and they can be updated of new articles which come out on the feed. Here is the Feed class:

```php
1  <?php
2
3  class Feed implements SplSubject
4  {
5      private $name;
6      private $observers = array();
7      private $content;
8
9      public function __construct($name)
10     {
11         $this->name = $name;
12     }
13
14     public function attach(SplObserver $observer)
15     {
16         $observerHash = spl_object_hash($observer);
17         $this->observers[$observerHash] = $observer;
18     }
19
20     public function detach(SplObserver $observer)
21     {
22         $observerHash = spl_object_hash($observer);
23         unset($this->observers[$observerHash]);
24     }
```

```
25
26      public function breakOutNews($content)
27      {
28          $this->content = $content;
29          $this->notify();
30      }
31
32      public function getContent()
33      {
34          return $this->content . " on " . $this->name . ".";
35      }
36
37      public function notify()
38      {
39          foreach ($this->observers as $value) {
40              $value->update($this);
41          }
42      }
43  }
```

When a `Reader` is `attach()`ed to the `Feed`, it is effectively added to an array of observers which then notify the class when the `breakOutNews()` function is run. The observers are stored in a key-value array. The key is effectively created by using the `spl_object_hash()` function which returns a unique hash ID for the object (note that the hash ID can be re-used when the object is destroyed).

The `Reader` class implements the `SplObserver` interface:

```
1   <?php
2
3   class Reader implements SplObserver
4   {
5       private $name;
6
7       public function __construct($name)
8       {
9           $this->name = $name;
10      }
11
12      public function update(\SplSubject $subject)
13      {
14          echo $this->name . ' is reading post ' . $subject->getContent() . " \n";
15      }
16  }
```

Here's a simple `index.php` class to utilise the Observer Pattern:

```php
1   <?php
2
3   require_once('Feed.php');
4   require_once('Reader.php');
5
6   $blog = new Feed('Junade.com');
7
8   $rhona = new Reader('Rhona');
9   $lillie = new Reader('Lillie');
10  $caitlin = new Reader('Caitlin');
11
12  //add reader
13  $blog->attach($rhona);
14  $blog->attach($lillie);
15  $blog->attach($caitlin);
16
17  //remove reader
18  $blog->detach($lillie);
19
20  //set break outs
21  $blog->breakOutNews('Object-Oriented PHP Book');
```

This script therefore outputs the following:

```
1   Rhona is reading post Object-Oriented PHP Book on Junade.com.
2   Caitlin is reading post Object-Oriented PHP Book on Junade.com.
```

The Observer pattern allows an easy and effective way for an Observer object to notify it's defendants (known as Subjects) of a change, this effectively allows us to distribute event handling throughout an application.

Conclusion

In this chapter we've covered the fundamentals of Design Patterns. There are many more Design Patterns both expressed in both the original *Gang of Four* Design Patterns book and in subsequent publications (such as *Code Complete*), however in this chapter we've discussed the fundamental ones to get you up and running.

In the next chapter we will discuss the importance of testing in reliable code and how testing can help make our code resilient to the forces of change.

Testing

The SweBoK (Software Engineering Body of Knowledge) defines some core processes involved in Software Engineering. Amongst them the topics of design, construction and testing are mentioned. Without effective design, the software cannot be constructed in a way which it delivers features in a reliable fashion. Without testing, the no one knows if the software will or will not work.

What good is software if it doesn't work? We are fundamentally hired as software engineers to deliver business value, not create cool looking code in funky languages. We should seek to build software that can demonstrably work, that's why we create automated tests - so we have proof that the software works as expected.

"But why is it necessary to *prove* it works?", I hear you cry. "I *just know* my software works." Let's take a simple example, refactoring. You come across some messy old code with half the program written in a single function and you want to refactor that code such that it is easier for you to build upon. When you are refactoring or building that additional functionality, what proof do you have that your software will work as before? When you add new functionality, how are you sure that new shiny stuff will not break existing functionality?

Well, you could manually go through a bunch of test cases on your own in a very time consuming way, but this wouldn't scale very well. Chances are you would lack rigor and it'd slow down your development process having to do this every time you want to merge a Pull Request.

Thankfully we can automate testing, we can automatically test features within our codebase to ensure they work as expected by writing the expected behavior as code.

Unit Testing

Unit Testing allows us to test units of our system individually, within the context of Object-Oriented PHP this means that we are actually testing the public methods of a given class in our system.

Let's started with a simple `composer.json` file which we can create and then run `composer install --dev` when we're good to go:

```
1   {
2     "require": {
3       "php": ">7.0.0"
4     },
5     "require-dev": {
6       "phpunit/phpunit": "5.5.0"
7     },
8     "autoload": {
9       "psr-4": {
10        "IcyApril\\Six\\": "src"
11      }
12    }
13  }
```

We have included PHPUnit in our dev dependencies, so let's include a `phpunit.xml` configuration file alongside our `composer.json` file that let's PHPUnit know where everything is:

```
1   <?xml version="1.0" encoding="UTF-8"?>
2   <phpunit bootstrap="vendor/autoload.php">
3       <testsuites>
4           <testsuite name="Six Test Suite">
5               <directory suffix=".php">./tests/</directory>
6           </testsuite>
7       </testsuites>
8       <filter>
9           <whitelist processUncoveredFilesFromWhitelist="true">
10              <directory suffix=".php">./src/</directory>
11          </whitelist>
12      </filter>
13  </phpunit>
```

We bootstrap PHPUnit to use our Composer autoload script, we tell it where our test suites live (including the file suffix and the directory where the tests live). The file also includes a whitelist to the directory of code we want to test.

Let's next create an `src` folder with some code for us to test, first let's create a simple `Storage` interface:

```php
1   <?php
2
3   namespace IcyApril\Six;
4
5   interface Storage
6   {
7       public function __construct(string $path);
8
9       public function storeContents(string $value): bool;
10
11      public function getContents(): string;
12  }
```

We can then implement this interface in a simple File class that allows us to store and recover data from the file system:

```php
1   <?php
2
3   namespace IcyApril\Six;
4
5
6   class File implements Storage
7   {
8       private $path;
9
10      public function __construct(string $path)
11      {
12          if (file_exists($path) === false) {
13              throw new FileException('File does not exist.');
14          }
15
16          $this->path = $path;
17      }
18
19      public function storeContents(string $value): bool
20      {
21          return file_put_contents($this->path, $value);
22      }
23
24      public function getContents(): string
25      {
26          $contents = file_get_contents($this->path);
```

```
27
28              if ($contents === false) {
29                  throw new FileException('Could not get contents (file may no longer \
30   exist).');
31              }
32
33          return $contents;
34      }
35
36  }
```

Note that we used a `FileException` in this class, so let's go ahead and create that exception class:

```
1   <?php
2
3   namespace IcyApril\Six;
4
5
6   class FileException extends \Exception
7   {
8
9   }
```

So we have a working `File` class in place now so we can create a tests folder and our first `FileTest` Unit Test class. So let's write some tests and then let's work through what they do:

```
1   <?php
2
3   use IcyApril\Six\File;
4
5   class FileTest extends PHPUnit_Framework_TestCase
6   {
7       public function testConstructor()
8       {
9           $fileLocation = tempnam(sys_get_temp_dir(), '');
10          $fileExists = new File($fileLocation);
11
12          $fileLocation = $fileLocation . 'NoExist';
13          $this->expectException(\IcyApril\Six\FileException::class);
14          $noExist = new File($fileLocation);
15      }
16
```

```
17      public function testStoreContents()
18      {
19          $fileLocation = tempnam(sys_get_temp_dir(), '');
20          $store = new File($fileLocation);
21          $stored = $store->storeContents('Hello, hello.');
22          $this->assertEquals('Hello, hello.', file_get_contents($fileLocation));
23          $this->assertEquals(true, $stored);
24
25          $stored = $store->storeContents('Welcome back.');
26          $this->assertEquals('Welcome back.', file_get_contents($fileLocation));
27          $this->assertEquals(true, $stored);
28      }
29
30      public function testGetContents()
31      {
32          $fileLocation = tempnam(sys_get_temp_dir(), '');
33          file_put_contents($fileLocation, 'Hello, hello.');
34          $store = new File($fileLocation);
35          $this->assertEquals('Hello, hello.', $store->getContents());
36
37          file_put_contents($fileLocation, 'Welcome back.');
38          $this->assertEquals('Welcome back.', $store->getContents());
39      }
40  }
```

The first method here is a testConstructor() method (all test methods must start with test to run, just like all test classes must be suffixed with Test), this method simply checks that an exception is thrown when a file does not exist and no exception is thrown when a file does not exist. In order to do this we are using tempnam() (create temporary directory) and sys_get_temp_dir() (get the system temporary file folder) functions.

The second method is the testStoreContents() method which we use to test the storeContent() method by creating files with various pieces of content using the storeContent() method and checking the correct contents are returned when checked with the file_get_contents()` function.

The third method, testGetContents(), tests the getContents() method by using the file_put_contents() function to write to a temporary file and seeing what's returned using the getContents() method.

We can run these Unit Tests simply by running:

```
1   $ ./vendor/bin/phpunit
```

Here's the output indicating all the tests have passed successfully:

```
junades-mbp:6 junade$ ./vendor/bin/phpunit
PHPUnit 5.5.0 by Sebastian Bergmann and contributors.

...                                                       3 / 3 (100%)

Time: 112 ms, Memory: 4.00MB

OK (3 tests, 7 assertions)
junades-mbp:6 junade$
```

Test Driven Development is a development process whereby the unit test is written for the software to pass, before developing the software. When the small unit of code is written, the software is written and then the Unit Tests are run - the code is then constantly refactored until the software passes the test.

Mocking

Let's suppose we have a JSON class that utilizes Storage interface via Dependency Injection; it is a simple class that encodes and decodes objects into JSON data for use by the Storage class:

```php
1   <?php
2
3   namespace IcyApril\Six;
4
5   class JSON
6   {
7       private $storage;
8
9       public function __construct(Storage $storage)
10      {
11          $this->storage = $storage;
12      }
13
14      public function store(\stdClass $object)
15      {
16          $json = json_encode($object);
17
18          if ($json === false) {
19              throw new JSONException('Could not encode JSON.');
20          }
21
22          return $this->storage->storeContents($json);
23      }
24
25      public function retrieve(): \stdClass
26      {
27          $contents = $this->storage->getContents();
28
29          if (empty($contents)) {
30              return new \stdClass();
31          }
32
33          $data = json_decode($contents);
34
35          if (json_last_error() > 0) {
36              throw new JSONException('Could not decode JSON.');
37          }
38
39          return $data;
40      }
41  }
```

So, we want to test this class but we don't want to make the tests so brittle that we have to test the underlying tests alongside them. This is where mocking comes into play, we can create fake classes we can test against. Before we get into the code, note that if a PHPUnit test class contains a setUp() method, that method is run before each individual test.

```php
1   <?php
2
3   class JSONTest extends PHPUnit_Framework_TestCase
4   {
5       private $storage;
6
7       protected function setUp()
8       {
9           $this->storage = $this->getMockBuilder(\IcyApril\Six\File::class)
10              ->disableOriginalConstructor()
11              ->getMock();
12      }
13
14      public function testStore()
15      {
16          $objectToStore = new stdClass();
17          $objectToStore->data = "hello.";
18
19          $this->storage
20              ->expects($this->once())
21              ->method('storeContents')
22              ->with('{"data":"hello."}')
23              ->willReturn(true);
24
25          $jsonStore = new \IcyApril\Six\JSON($this->storage);
26          $stored = $jsonStore->store($objectToStore);
27
28          $this->assertTrue($stored);
29      }
30
31      public function testRetrieve()
32      {
33          $objectToRetrieve = new stdClass();
34          $objectToRetrieve->data = "hello.";
35
36          $this->storage
37              ->expects($this->once())
38              ->method('getContents')
39              ->willReturn('{"data":"hello."}');
```

```
40
41        $jsonRetrieve = new \IcyApril\Six\JSON($this->storage);
42        $retrieved = $jsonRetrieve->retrieve();
43
44        $this->assertEquals($objectToRetrieve, $retrieved);
45    }
46
47    public function testRetrieveNoData()
48    {
49        $this->storage
50            ->expects($this->once())
51            ->method('getContents')
52            ->willReturn('');
53
54        $jsonRetrieve = new \IcyApril\Six\JSON($this->storage);
55        $retrieved = $jsonRetrieve->retrieve();
56
57        $this->assertEquals(new stdClass(), $retrieved);
58    }
59
60    public function testRetrieveCorrupt()
61    {
62        $this->storage
63            ->expects($this->once())
64            ->method('getContents')
65            ->willReturn('this is fake[ json ]]]]]');
66
67        $jsonRetrieve = new \IcyApril\Six\JSON($this->storage);
68
69        $this->expectException(\IcyApril\Six\JSONException::class);
70        $jsonRetrieve->retrieve();
71    }
72 }
```

When adding methods to each of the mocks we are able to specify with the expects() parameter how many times the function will be run, what it will return with the willReturn() method and there is also a with() option to define what parameters the method should be called with. The test will fail should any of these criteria not be met.

If we run these tests again, you can see these Unit Tests being run:

```
junades-mbp:6 junade$ ./vendor/bin/phpunit
PHPUnit 5.5.0 by Sebastian Bergmann and contributors.

.......                                                       7 / 7 (100%)

Time: 84 ms, Memory: 4.00MB

OK (7 tests, 15 assertions)
junades-mbp:6 junade$
```

Integration Testing

Look back at the code example in the last section; let's imagine we didn't use Mocking and instead directly injected a real File class for the JSON class to consume. We'd be testing the modules *together*, in essence we'd be testing how the modules fit together instead of them individually.

This is *Integration Testing*, we are testing how classes are wired together. This has it's uses, but note that the integration test suite should be kept apart from the unit test suite; failure to do this will result in the tests not checking individual class units work before running integration tests.

End-to-End Tests

Sometimes you need to test the interface to your application for end-to-end testing when Integration Testing or Unit Testing isn't enough. These kinds of tests aim to test your entire application fits together, not just one or two class units.

If you're testing an API you can pull in a HTTP client like Guzzle (composer require guzzle/guzzle --dev) or you can utilize a headless browser like Selenium if you're still rendering HTML pages directly. Once done, you can then utilize that library to build HTTP queries against your API or test your UI like a real browser.

```
1   <?php
2
3   class UserAgentTest extends PHPUnit_Framework_TestCase
4   {
5       private $http;
6
7       public function setUp()
8       {
9           $this->http = new GuzzleHttp\Client(['base_uri' => 'https://httpbin.org/\
10  ']);
11      }
12
13      public function tearDown()
14      {
15          $this->http = null;
16      }
17
18      public function testGet()
19      {
20          $response = $this->http->request('GET', 'user-agent');
21
22          $this->assertEquals(200, $response->getStatusCode());
23
24          $contentType = $response->getHeaders()["Content-Type"][0];
25          $this->assertEquals("application/json", $contentType);
26
27          $userAgent = json_decode($response->getBody())->{"user-agent"};
28          $this->assertRegexp('/Guzzle/', $userAgent);
29      }
30
31      public function testPut()
32      {
33          $response = $this->http->request('PUT', 'user-agent', ['http_errors' => \
34  false]);
35
36          $this->assertEquals($response->getStatusCode(), 405);
37      }
38  }
```

Here is a simple test class that uses the setUp method to create a Guzzle HTTP client and tearDown to remove it after each test has run. With this API client in place we are testing with a HTTP GET request that the /user-agent endpoint returns a 200 OK HTTP status code, the response type is application/json and the body contains the phrase Guzzle (our User Agent). We then do the same with a HTTP `PUT` request which tests to see if we get a `405 Method Not Allowed` when we try to send a `PUT` request to a `GET` endpoint. This can be extended to all HTTP methods on a particular endpoint.

Conclusion (Testing Matters!)

Without testing we cannot reliably refactor code, and we waste time manually testing the new features we add to a codebase. In cases where SOLID Principles are not followed we cannot even guarantee the security of existing features within our codebase.

Other testing methods have recently emerged, BDD for example lets us write our tests in plain-English to assert whether a piece of functionality is or isn't embedded into a piece of software; however before learning new techniques it is vital you understand the basics of Unit Testing.

Software Testing, contrary to popular belief, does not slow down the development of software - it in fact accelerates it and safeguards the quality of what you build. It provides, in code, documentation for what your software should do.

How to Write Better code

Refactoring

The existing design of software may not necessarily match the existing or future purpose of software. Refactoring exists to help us resolve this discrepancy. We can, in effect, change the design of existing software.

Like most PHP Developers, part of my career was built on the need to refactor legacy code to counter technical debt. Due to bad design in software, delivering value to the client became ever more difficult and stressful until bad design decisions were rectified. For developers working on badly designed projects, making repayments on technical debt, whilst also delivering value is a key skill - in this concluding chapter I'd like to explain how it is possible to square-the-circle and both deliver value whilst paying down technical debt.

There are multiple bad practice approaches which can lead to a project being filled with technical debt; for example, source code with a complex and tangled control structure can be referred to as "Spaghetti Code". I remember a colleague once exclaiming "I have so much spaghetti, I could open an Italian restaurant!"

Martin Fowler used the following pseudo-graph (plotting delivered functionality vs time on two stereotypical programming projects) to describe the phenomenon of technical debt[4]:

---

[4]http://martinfowler.com/bliki/DesignStaminaHypothesis.html

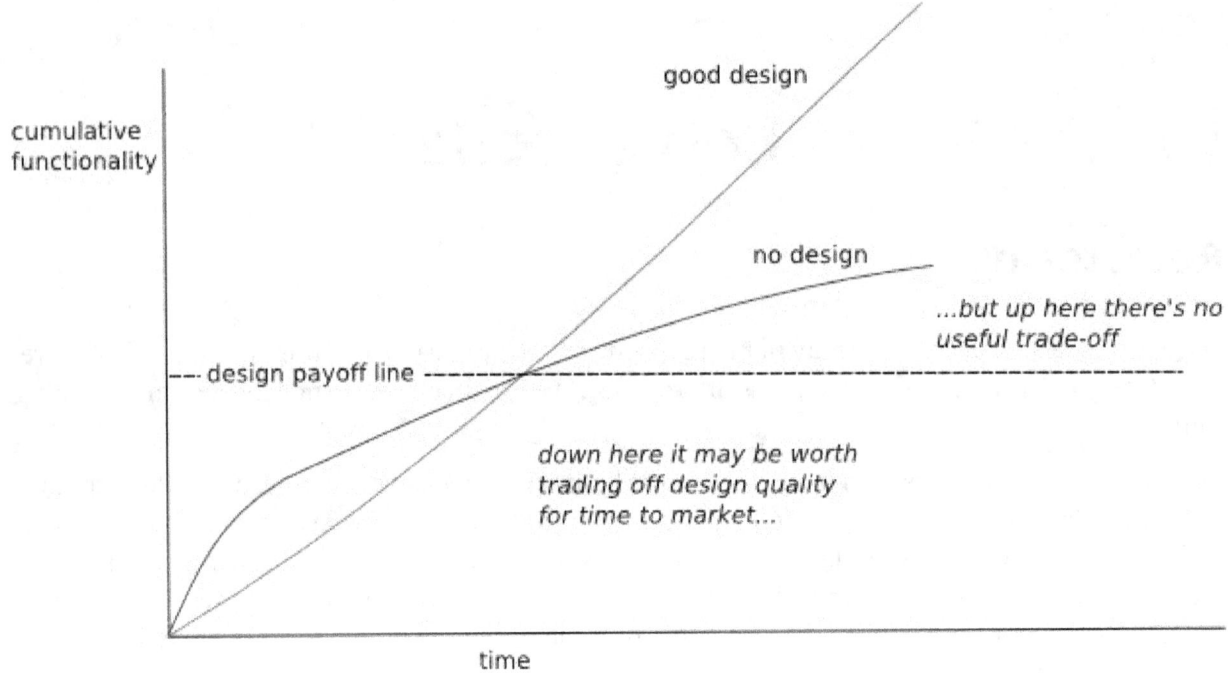

Design Stamina Graph

Short-term, the software project with no design is able to yield slightly more code in a time constrained environment, however once the "design payoff line" is passed - the project with well designed code is able to deliver functionality far faster.

As more functionality is delivered, the codebase with no design deteriorates, meaning it is harder to modify and deliver valuable functionality. To the contrary, the project with good design is able to maintain a linear delivery of valuable functionality, by maintaining great design through Agile practices. Fundamentally technical debt damages your ability to deliver value to your client.

The cost of never paying down this technical debt is clear; eventually the cost to deliver functionality will become so slow that it is easy for a well-designed competitive software product to overtake the badly-designed software in terms of features. In my experience, badly designed software can also lead to a more stressed engineering workforce, in turn leading higher staff churn (which in turn affects costs and productivity when delivering features). Additionally, due to the complexity in a given codebase, the ability to accurately estimate work will also disappear. In cases where development agencies charge on an feature-to-feature basis, the profit margin for delivering code will eventually deteriorate.

Testing

Before refactoring any code, we have to ensure that we don't cause damage or waste time by introducing bugs. Not only can these cause bugs going into production, they can also cost time having to constantly play whack-a-mole with bugs. Being careful and guessing software will continue to function is simply not enough - we need a scientific way to test software works before deploying. Additionally it provides for a tangible, executable specification of what our software should do.

Manual testing is simply too prone to not being thorough, additionally it is time consuming and far too costly. In order to be effective, tests which can be automated should be automated.

Automated testing is often described with a pyramid similar to the one displayed below, with Unit Tests being the largest in quantity to the bottom with manual session based tests being the very fewest at the top of the pyramid:

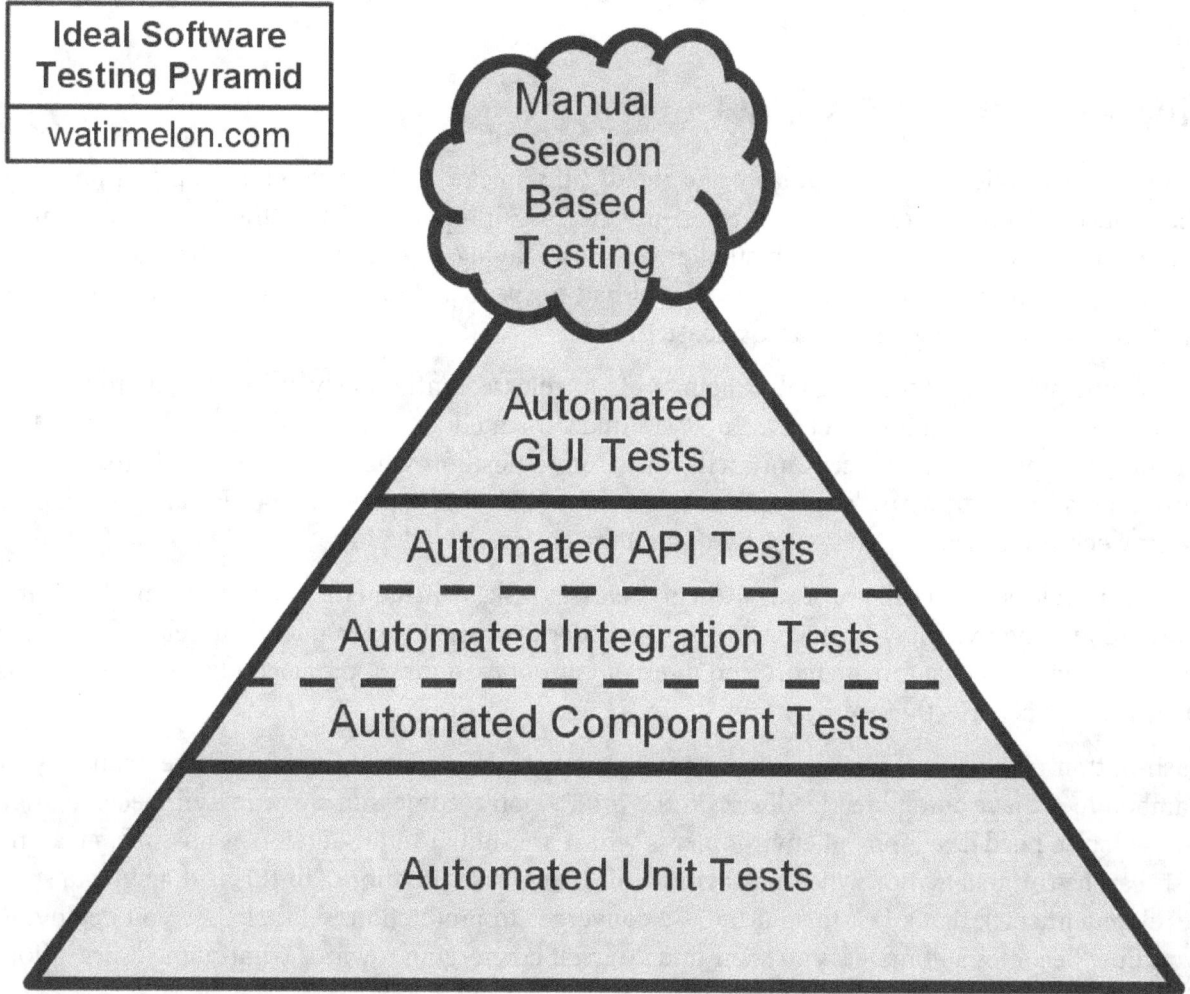

Ideal Automated Testing Pyramid

Unfortunately we can't reach this ideal easily - there is some really messy PHP out there. There are cases where it is hard to implement Unit Tests in PHP before refactoring starts, instead we can start automating things like GUI tests or API tests. Any app, regardless of how bad its codebase is, can have some automated testing baked in.

The PHPUnit framework has support for browser regression testing through Selenium WebDriver.

By using PHPUnit with Selenium you are able to automatically run browser-level tests for your application, which can provide an indication as to what has or hasn't broken. PHPUnit have put together great documentation on using PHPUnit with Selenium[5], it is even possible to capture a browser screenshot when a given test fails. Similarly, if you're refactoring an API backend, you can use PHPUnit together with a HTTP client like Guzzle to create Automated API Tests.

You may be desperate to go in and start tidying up the codebase as it stands, but adding these tests will ultimately allow you to reach a faster speed when doing so. As the refactoring code converges to a more Object-Oriented or functional design, you can start adding low-level Unit Tests which provide much faster feedback.

Speed up the Release Train

You need to be able to release regularly and rapidly. If you can't do this, you have a major problem. The chances of releases encountering problems increases proportionally to the amount of change you deploy; less can go wrong with smaller releases. Having a regular release schedule is vital to countering technical debt - much of the effort I had to spend with new clients was breaking down the barriers to achieving a systematic release train.

You should start with the end goal of being able to release continuously, whenever there is value to be added by performing a release. In 2011 Amazon stated they were able to deploy every 11.6 seconds, though you almost certainly will start from a position where you aren't able to. I would recommend you start by picking a day of the week where you deploy (no, not Friday) and deploy every week from then on. No matter how small the change, you deploy.

Once your release train can cruise on a weekly release track, switch up the speed and start deploying more frequently; twice a week and then daily. In order to achieve this frequency in releases you will find that you need to automate more and more of your operational approach and converge towards DevOps. This is perfectly healthy.

Push-button releases will require further automation work, implementing a tool like TeamCity or Bamboo to achieve automated feedback on the production readiness of software will become vital. You will also need development environments which are similar to production as possible, meaning tests can be run in a manor which will avoid lethal edge-case situations. To this end, having a solid development stack that's fast to spin-up and converges to production will help. As you deploying workflow becomes automated, you soon find yourself converging towards Continuous Integration.

Preventing damage is merely one benefit of Continuous Integration, in the book *"A Practical Approach to Large-Scale Agile Development: How HP Transformed LaserJet FutureSmart Firmware"* it is demonstrated that by implementing CI at HP overall development costs reduced by ~40%, programs under development increased by ~140%, development costs per program reduced by 78% and resources driving innovation increased by 5x. Simplifying the software release process allows developers to focus on writing code and delivering value instead of boring and repetitive release processes.

---

[5]https://phpunit.de/manual/4.8/en/selenium.html

Continuous delivery is a set of principles and practices to reduce the cost, time, and risk of delivering incremental changes to users. – Definition of Continuous Delivery by Martin Fowler

Automation of repetitive tasks is an excellent practice, humans are the most fallible part of the development process. Preventing a developer from manually having to enter dangerous commands into an SSH terminal will help your deployment operational resilience.

What to Refactor?

As you run through the code, it is vital you understand what to refactor - to avoid inserting Anti-Patterns which take the codebase in the wrong direction. Anti-Patterns act as negative solutions towards recurring solutions, whereas refactoring towards Design Patterns provides a positive resolution to recurring problems. Code Smells are often used to find bad practices which root themselves in deep design issues within the software. Issues may also reside outside the codebase itself, architectural issues will need to be resolved through the implementation of well-suited Architectural Patterns.

To start with it is often a great idea to get your code in shape so you can start adding Unit Tests. The process of making your code more testable can usually also help iron out some core issues. For example; restricting the use of global states within your application won't just help make it more testable, but will also make it more resilient and easier to change.

Ensuring your application converges to Object-Orientation is also a great step, extracting smaller methods from a massively bloated functions allows us to prevent code reuse. It is a great idea to ensure your code complies with the SOLiD principles we discussed earlier in this book.

In particular, approaches such as favoring composition over inheritance and programming to interfaces rather than implementations will serve you well. With the basics of Object-Orientation nailed down, you can start moving Anti-Pattern behavior towards better suited Design Patterns. For example; replacing hard-coded notifications with the Observer Design Pattern or replacing one/many distinctions with the Composite Design Pattern.

Code Smells

The book "Refactoring: Improving the Design of Existing Code" by Martin Fowler provides some great information on identifying Code Smells how you can resolve them (though note that this book is not PHP specific). In this book Fowler provides a definition for Code Smells: "a code smell is a surface indication that usually corresponds to a deeper problem in the system".

They do not indicate software bugs as such, but instead indicate software design issues. These issues can increase the risk of introducing bugs later on in the development process or result in failure later down the road, additionally they can slow down the development of software by making the codebase less resilient to the forces of change.

Here are some examples of the most common Code Smells you're likely to encounter:

- *Duplicated Code* - identical or very similar code repeated throughout the codebase that should be abstracted into a single method. This should be avoided and the DRY (Don't Repeat Yourself) principle should be followed instead.
- *Contrived Complexity* - building software with a degree of complexity that isn't required for the functionality being built, instead the KISS (Keep It Simple Stupid) principle should be followed.
- *Large Class* - a class that has grown unsustainably large, they will often not follow the Single Responsibility Principle.
- *Inappropriate Intimacy* - a class that depends closely on the implementation details of another class when it should instead depend on an abstraction.
- *Long Method* - a method that has grown too large (usually over 10 lines long) and no longer completes a single function but seeks to lock up far too much business logic in a single method. Instead the separate pieces of logic should be abstracted to private methods in the same class.
- *Poor Naming* - obfuscating the purpose of a method, class or variable by poorly naming it. A developer should be easily able to understand what something does or what role it plays through it's name.
- *Developer Code Fragment* - functions like `var_dump()` and `print_r()` are left in the codebase when it's deployed.
- *Excessive Fields* - excessive fields in a method or the constructor of a class causing confusion when instantiating a class or using a method. This cab be refactored to the Builder design pattern.

PHP-MD

PHP-MD isn't a PHP-based doctor, but is instead a neat too allowing you to identify Code Smells within your codebase automatically. In order to start using this, you can run `composer require phpmd/phpmd --dev` in a Composer project.

Now if you check my `composer.json` file you'll see `"phpmd/phpmd": "^2.6"` in the development dependencies:

```
1   {
2       "name": "icyapril/tail",
3       "description": "PHP library seeking to mimic the Unix tail program.",
4       "type": "library",
5       "require": {
6           "php": ">7.0.0"
7       },
8       "require-dev": {
9           "phpunit/phpunit": "5.5.0",
10          "codeclimate/php-test-reporter": "dev-master",
```

```
11          "phpmd/phpmd": "^2.6"
12      },
13      "license": "BSD-3-Clause",
14      "authors": [
15          {
16              "name": "Junade Ali",
17              "email": "mjsa@junade.com"
18          }
19      ],
20      "autoload": {
21          "psr-4": {
22              "IcyApril\\Tail\\": "src"
23          }
24      },
25      "scripts": {
26          "test": "phpunit"
27      }
28  }
```

You may need to run `composer install --dev` to install all your development dependencies, however with all the dev dependencies installed you can now run PHP-MD to find out some Code Smells.

```
1  $ ./vendor/bin/phpmd ./src/ text cleancode,codesize,controversial,design,naming,\
2  unusedcode
3  /Users/junade/Documents/oophp-book/phpBook2Code/7/Tail/src/File.php:60        The metho\
4  d getLastLines has a boolean flag argument $adaptive, which is a certain sign of\
5   a Single Responsibility Principle violation.
6  /Users/junade/Documents/oophp-book/phpBook2Code/7/Tail/src/File.php:122       The meth\
7  od getBuffer has a boolean flag argument $adaptive, which is a certain sign of a\
8   Single Responsibility Principle violation.
```

After calling the binary for PHP-MD, the first argument is the directory of the source code we want to search, the second argument is the format of the report (available options are xml, text, html) and finally the last is a comma separated of the rules we want to run against (I have included a comma seperated list of all the default available rules, you can write your own in XML).

The output is a line-by-line list of the Code Smells within the codebase which can give you an indication as to where technical debt lies.

Deliver Value

Businesses are built on the need to deliver value to clients - one of the massive benefits of refactoring over total rewrites is the fact that you can continue to add value to your existing codebase whilst refactoring it.

When starting to work on an existing part of the codebase, it is perfectly acceptable to start by adding tests (to accelerate the development of software). With these in place, when encountering a new part of a codebase, refactoring will help you gain an understanding how the codebase operates, and will indeed allow you to take the simplest route to achieve your intended logic.

Mitigating Technical Debt through refactoring your codebase doesn't slow down development, to the contrary it speeds it up.

> Refactor mercilessly to keep the design simple as you go and to avoid needless clutter and complexity. Keep your code clean and concise so it is easier to understand, modify, and extend. Make sure everything is expressed once and only once. In the end it takes less time to produce a system that is well groomed.

– "Refactor Mercilessly[6]" is a key principle of Extreme Programming.

Recognize Institutional Problems

You may often find the problem with bad code rooted in organizational failures within your company. It is vital to ensure you that you not only achieve buy-in for refactoring, but that the process is not hindered by cargo-cult practices or internal political disputes. This may well mean you have to have a heart-to-heart conversation with your manager to ensure these barriers are removed.

Badly implemented Scrum is often known of railroading proper engineering practices, no matter which management methodology you subscribe to - the need to subscribe to proper engineering practices is vital. Without ensuring code is properly tested or that code is constantly refactored, you risk falling back into the same trap of technical debt. I would highly recommend reviewing the practices described in Extreme Programming to see what you can implement from there.

Conclusion

In this concluding chapter of this book we have summarized how technical debt can be found and repaired by identifying Code Smells and refactoring it to be inline with modern standards. Through utilizing well conceived Design Patterns we are able to instead refactor our code in a way which is extensible and flexible.

Throughout this book we have discussed how you can build software that is well-designed and resilient to the forces of change, in order to enact such changes (whether on your own codebase or one you've inherited) on your codebase you can utilize refactoring.

---

[6]http://www.extremeprogramming.org/rules/refactor.html

www.ingramcontent.com/pod-product-compliance
Lightning Source LLC
Chambersburg PA
CBHW081153180526
45170CB00006B/2065